HADRIAN'S WALL

THE LANDMARK LIBRARY

Chapters in the History of Civilization

The Landmark Library is a record of the achievements of humankind from the late Stone Age to the present day. Each volume in the series is devoted to a crucial theme in the history of civilization, and offers a concise and authoritative text accompanied by a generous complement of images. Contributing authors to The Landmark Library are chosen for their ability to combine scholarship with a flair for communicating their specialist knowledge to a wider, non-specialist readership.

IN THE SERIES

Guernica, James Attlee
Eroica: The First Great Romantic Symphony, James Hamilton-Paterson
Magna Carta, Dan Jones
Messiah, Jonathan Keates
Stonehenge, Francis Pryor

FORTHCOMING VOLUMES

Skyscraper, Dan Cruickshank
The British Museum, James Hamilton
Dante's Divine Comedy, Ian Thomson
The Sarpedon Krater, Nigel Spivey
Versailles, Colin Jones
City of Light: The Rebuilding of Paris, Rupert Christiansen
The Royal Society, Adrian Tinniswood
The Rite of Spring, Gillian Moore
The Plays of Shakespeare, Peter Conrad

HADRIAN'S WALL

ADRIAN GOLDSWORTHY

HEAD of ZEUS

First published in 2018
by Head of Zeus Ltd

A CIP catalogue record for this book is available from the British Library.

ISBN (HB) 978 1784974725
(E) 9781784974718

Designed by Isambard Thomas
Printed in Spain by Graficas Estella

Head of Zeus Ltd
First Floor East
5–8 Hardwick Street
London EC1R 4RG

WWW.HEADOFZEUS.COM

previous page

Hadrian's Wall in the snow. This is milecastle 42 at Cawfields, one of the best-preserved examples of these small fortlets spaced at every Roman mile along the Wall.

Birrens

Bewcastle

Hous

Netherby

Great
Chesters

Birdoswald

Carvoran

Castlesteads

Bowness

Drumburgh

Stanwix

Burgh
by Sands

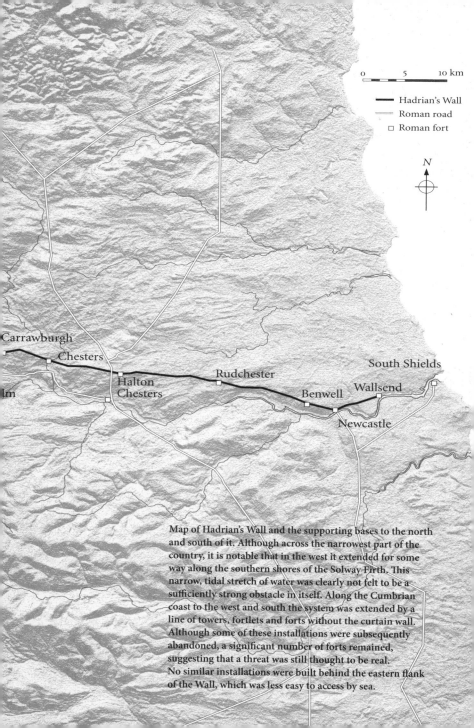

0   5   10 km

— Hadrian's Wall
— Roman road
□ Roman fort

N

Carrawburgh

Chesters

Halton
Chesters

lm

Rudchester

South Shields

Benwell   Wallsend

Newcastle

Map of Hadrian's Wall and the supporting bases to the north and south of it. Although across the narrowest part of the country, it is notable that in the west it extended for some way along the southern shores of the Solway Firth. This narrow, tidal stretch of water was clearly not felt to be a sufficiently strong obstacle in itself. Along the Cumbrian coast to the west and south the system was extended by a line of towers, fortlets and forts without the curtain wall. Although some of these installations were subsequently abandoned, a significant number of forts remained, suggesting that a threat was still thought to be real. No similar installations were built behind the eastern flank of the Wall, which was less easy to access by sea.

INTRODUCTION

'Just when you think you are at the world's end, you see a smoke
from East to West as far as the eye can turn, and then, under it,
also as far as the eye can stretch, houses and temples, shops and
theatres, barracks and granaries, trickling along like dice behind –
always behind – one long, low, rising and falling, and hiding and
showing line of towers. And that is the Wall!'

'Ah!' said the children, taking breath.

'You may well,' said Parnesius.
'Old men who have followed the Eagles since boyhood say nothing
in the Empire is more wonderful than first sight of the Wall!'[1]

I suspect that hearing my father read these words to my brother
and me at bedtime was the first time that I 'saw' the Wall.
These days Kipling is not very fashionable, so I wonder how
many children hear or read *Puck of Pook's Hill*, but I remember
loving these stories of English history, and most of all the three
chapters when Parnesius, centurion of the Thirtieth Legion, tells
his story. The Romans have always had an appeal for me that is
hard to explain, although part of it is that they came to where
I lived, which made them somehow more real and part of 'my'
history.

Parnesius was a likeable hero, as much a first-rate British
subaltern in late nineteenth-century India as he was a Roman
officer, and his story was full of wars and battle, which always
have a great pull on a boy's imagination. Reading the story now,
some of it is odd, such as the appearance of the 'winged hats' –
Vikings a few centuries early – to dominate the Picts and lead
them against Hadrian's Wall, which they then try to capture tower
by tower. Yet, as is often the case with Kipling, there are moments

where you still feel that he found the essence of a time or place, and this passage is one of them. His Wall is a bit higher than the real thing, while so far there is no trace of a Roman theatre along it, and we now know that by the late fourth century, when the story is set, the civilian settlements outside forts were greatly diminished or had vanished altogether, and most of the turrets had been demolished. Even so, the picture he paints of a bustling, raucous community of soldiers and civilians drawn from all of the empire and now living on its distant northern frontier probably contains a lot of truth for much of the Wall's history.

In the years after hearing Parnesius's story, I have read more about the Wall, starting while still very young with the Ladybird *Julius Caesar and Roman Britain*, where I crossed out the H from the label on the maps behind its front and back covers to rename the structure 'Adrian's Wall'. At the time this seemed hilarious. Later I moved on to ever more serious and scholarly works. My first visit came after wheedling my parents into diverting from the quickest route on the return journey from a family holiday in the north of Scotland. Decades later, I am still reading and still learning, and have visited sites on the Wall many times, but that first glimpse described by Parnesius to the children in the story is always at the back of my mind. Hadrian's Wall is special, not only to those of us interested in Ancient Rome and the Roman army, but more widely.

Hadrian's Wall stretched for some 73 miles (118 km) from coast to coast across northern Britain. Although this is impressive, in size it is dwarfed by the complex of fortifications making up what we know as the Great Wall of China, which was also in use for far longer than the 'mere' three centuries or so of Hadrian's Wall. The Wall lay on the fringe of Roman Britain, itself on the fringes of the Roman empire, the frontiers of which ran for thousands of miles, along great rivers, through mountains and deserts. Hadrian's Wall was one small component of the imperial

overleaf: This view of Housesteads fort from the air – looking westwards – gives an idea of the size of one of the bases along Hadrian's Wall.

border control and defence, and rarely would it have occupied the thoughts of the emperors who ruled this vast empire.

All this is true, but the Wall is still special because it is unlike any other Roman frontier. Nowhere else were the defences so elaborate or monumental in scale; nowhere else is there so much archaeology to see in so small an area. In a sense the Wall figures larger in our sense of the Roman world than it surely did to the Romans, much as provincial and rather vulgar Pompeii and the more sophisticated Herculaneum have done so much to shape our ideas of city life and art because of the catastrophe that led to their remarkable preservation. Since so much of the ancient world is lost for ever, the sites that survive often assume far greater importance than they ever possessed when they were living communities. In 1987 Hadrian's Wall was named a UNESCO World Heritage Site (incorporated into the broader Frontiers of the Roman Empire World Heritage Site in 2005), which acknowledged its importance. Over 90 per cent of it is now invisible on the ground, and yet even so it is the largest of the many monuments left by the Roman empire and one of the most famous.

It is also one of the most frequently visited, drawing people to walk the Hadrian's Wall Path or look at the excavated remains of forts and the Wall itself. If it lacks the intimate detail and dramatic story of Pompeii and Herculaneum, or the obvious history and importance of Rome itself, or the spectacle of theatres, amphitheatres, temples or aqueducts dotted around the old empire, still tens of thousands come every year to see it. Most go to the central sector, where more of the Wall is exposed and it snakes across a landscape of dramatic ridges and crags. It is very rare to see a photograph of other sections of the Wall, so that people are usually surprised to learn that for most of its length it crossed gentler rolling countryside, while in the far west its last few miles ran close to the sea along the shore of the Solway Firth.

The Wall itself was also part of a much larger network including military bases, towns and roads to the north and south, and the installations along the Cumbrian coast in the west. Occupied by the Romans for the best part of 300 years, generations of soldiers and civilians, of provincials and the local peoples lived their lives on and around the Wall and the broad military zone it created.

In most people's minds the purpose of any wall is fairly simple, especially one of the sheer size of Hadrian's Wall. A wall is a barrier, dividing one side from the other, and for many the idea persists that it was built 'to keep the Scots out' – or Picts, for those with slightly more sense of history. Hadrian's Wall can be seen as the end of the empire, where civilization stopped and barbarism began – although today's fashionable hostility to empires no doubt will incline many to sympathize more with the so-called barbarians.

Archaeologists know that the truth is different and a good deal more complicated, but will also admit that there is much about the Wall, its purpose and operation that we do not understand. Only a tiny fraction of the literature of the ancient world has survived into the modern era. These texts mention Hadrian's Wall no more than a handful of times, and the sole surviving statement about its purpose claims that Hadrian built the Wall 'to separate the barbarians from the Romans'. The comment is brief, and was written down some 200 years later by an author notorious for his inaccuracy and inventions, so that it is a sign of the extreme poverty of sources that we make use of it at all. It is only in recent years that we have evidence that it may indeed have been named after the emperor who ordered its construction, although using his family name Aelius rather than Hadrianus. The *Vallum Aelium* or 'Wall of Aelius' kept this name for only a generation or so, and afterwards was simply the *Vallum*.[2]

Hadrian's Wall can be understood only by examination of its physical remains, backed by inscriptions, finds from the sites along it, and comparison with what we understand of the Roman army and the Roman world from other places and sources. Yet no other Roman frontier was quite like Hadrian's Wall, making direct analogy difficult, while debates over its function strike to the heart of wider debates over how the Roman empire worked. Excavation has provided a lot of information, even though older reports are often frustratingly vague in their recording and the result of less sophisticated methods. Archaeology is expensive, while these days funding is in short supply and work on the Wall less fashionable than it deserves to be. Even so, where work occurs, it continues to throw up surprises which fundamentally alter our understanding of the Wall.

Frustratingly incomplete as our evidence is, we face an even greater problem because almost all of it deals solely with the Roman side of things. The Iron Age peoples living to the north of the Wall are poorly understood. Roman sources give us the names of tribes and some places, but we can never be sure whether these reflect the reality, since outsiders so often misunderstand other cultures. Far more settlements have been located than used to be known, suggesting that at least some parts of what would become Scotland were relatively densely populated, while environmental evidence suggests that some regions were also extensively cultivated for some of the Roman period. Iron Age sites are difficult to date with the sort of precision that might allow us to relate developments in settlement north of the Wall to the Roman frontier's purpose and day-to-day functioning.

We really do not know enough about the political and military practices of the tribes to describe the threat they posed to the Romans – or, for that matter, the threat the Romans posed to them. Wars were fought between the Romans and the tribes in the second, third and fourth centuries AD, but, as we shall see, very little is known about any of them. Raiding appears to have been common – perhaps universal – in Iron Age Europe,

The Rudge Cup is one of several bronze bowls which seem to have been
made as mementoes of Hadrian's Wall for soldiers or travellers to keep.
It has the names of several of the Wall forts running around the top.
In the centre are the letters BANNA, the Roman name for Birdoswald.

so we would expect to find this small-scale military activity in northern Britain, but extending what we know of 'Celtic' society elsewhere (which in itself comes largely from the viewpoint of Greco-Roman outsiders) to the peoples of the north must only be done with caution. Linguistic links may not necessarily reflect a common political and military culture, but in the end we simply do not know. Thus we must do our best to reconstruct the story of Hadrian's Wall, knowing that at the very best we have mere glimpses of only one side of the story. Whatever military threat existed – or was perceived by the Romans – can only be conjectured by looking at the methods they used to deal with it.

With Hadrian's Wall there are few definite answers, many theories and even more questions. This book cannot hope to explore them all in detail, but its aim is to give an idea of how scholars try to understand it and its place in the wider history of Roman Britain. Rather than qualify every statement, sometimes the book will reflect my own judgement on the most likely interpretation, but the works cited at the end will allow interested readers access to the considerable literature on each subject.

My central premise is that Hadrian's Wall and all the installations associated with it were intended to assist the Roman army performing the tasks assigned to it in northern Britain. Soldiers were not there to serve the Wall; the Wall was there to serve them. This may seem obvious, but there is always a danger that physical remains take over our thoughts at the expense of the human beings whose activities and lives leave less tangible reminders. The sheer scale and longevity of Hadrian's Wall make it clear that it performed a practical function and that – at least most of the time – it performed it well. That much we can say with confidence, but understanding just what that function was and how it developed over time is much like trying to put together a jigsaw puzzle when most of the pieces are missing and without the picture on the box to serve as a guide.

1 Roman mile = 1,618 yards or 0.92 imperial miles = 1.479 km.

Roman foot = 11.64 imperial inches = 29.6 cm.

Wall miles: In the twentieth century a scholarly convention was created to ease the identification of sections of Hadrian's Wall and the installations along it. This was based around numbering milecastles from 0 at Wallsend to 80 at Bowness-on-Solway. The stretch between each milecastle became a Wall mile, with Wall mile 1 beginning at Wallsend and extending westwards. All numbers of turrets and milecastles derive from this system.

Britannia:
outpost of empire

Britain was a late addition to the Roman empire, conquered at a time when expansion was becoming rare, but the actual conquest in AD 43 was not the first military contact between the empire and the Britons. Almost a century before, Julius Caesar, then proconsul or governor of Gaul, landed in the southeast in 55 and again in 54 BC. He beat down the fierce resistance of the local tribes, accepted their submission, but did not choose to stay over the winter and never returned. News of Caesar's expeditions to the mysterious, almost mythical island which lay out in the encircling oceans surrounding the three continents known to the Greeks and Romans was greeted at Rome with euphoria and public celebration – almost akin to the Moon landing in 1969. The Senate suspended public business for twenty days of official thanksgiving, an unprecedented celebration far grander than any awarded to mark victories in far more important wars in the past. Practical results and profits were less impressive. The orator Cicero noted that there was no silver, nor 'booty except for slaves; but I doubt we'll find any scribes or musicians amongst them'.[3]

Caesar was one of the gifted and ambitious commanders who conquered large swathes of territory on behalf of Rome's Republic. Rome was founded in the eighth century BC, at first one small Latin city among many. Over time it grew, displaying from very early on a unique talent for absorbing others. By the third century BC Rome controlled virtually all the Italian Peninsula, and hundreds of thousands of people who were not ethnically Latin, let alone 'Roman', were Roman citizens. Former enemies became allies and, after a generation or so, often citizens who shared in the responsibilities and profits of expansion. Rome's Republic was led in peace and war by elected magistrates, drawn from the wealthiest citizens and predominantly from a small group of aristocratic families. Former magistrates provided the bulk of the Senate, some 600 senior statesmen whose role was to advise and guide the magistrates and the popular assemblies who actually had the power to pass laws. The system was designed to prevent any individual or group from gaining permanent supreme power, which meant that many provincial governors went out to their provinces eager to win glory in the short time before they were replaced. Aggression and conquest were not constant, but over time the empire controlled by the Roman Republic grew. In the second century BC the Republic came to dominate the Mediterranean, and soon its legions advanced far from its shores. Conquest brought vast wealth and glory to a few of the aristocracy, raising them above their peers and putting a heavy strain on the system.

Men like Caesar greatly increased the pace of conquest, but they were also the leaders in the succession of civil wars that tore the Republican system of government apart. Most died violently, in Caesar's case stabbed to death at a meeting of the Senate. Civil war resumed soon afterwards, ending only when Mark Antony's suicide in 30 BC left Caesar's great-nephew and heir as the last remaining warlord. Caesar Augustus, as he was soon to be named, became Rome's first emperor, his power ultimately resting on control of the army. He styled himself as *princeps*, first citizen and first servant of the state, so that scholars refer to the rule of Rome's emperors as the principate. Ultimately his power rested on control of the army, a permanent, professional force of around 300,000 men, divided almost equally between the citizen soldiers of the legions and provincial and foreign auxiliaries. Every soldier swore an oath of loyalty to the *princeps*, and it was from the emperor that all pay and promotion came.

Augustus cleansed himself of his bloody rise to power by giving Romans and provincials internal peace and constant victory against foreign enemies. Almost everyone was desperate for stability and prosperity after decades of civil war and massacre, so that they were willing to accept the dominance of one man as better than any likely alternative. In spite of frequent severe

illnesses, Augustus outlived almost all his contemporaries, and over time everyone forgot the man who had slaughtered his way to the top and instead saw only the peacemaker and 'Father of his country'. Victories over foreign enemies made Rome safe, its empire wealthy, and were something that all patriotic Romans could celebrate, and Augustus provided a constant stream of such successes. By the time of his death Rome's empire was largely complete, bounded by the Atlantic in the west, the Rhine, the Danube and the Euphrates in the east, the Sahara desert in the south and the Channel coast in the north. Just before he died in AD 14, a little short of his seventy-seventh birthday, Augustus advised his successor to 'keep the empire within its present boundaries'. Whether or not he meant to bring a permanent halt to expansion or just give the empire a period of rest and recovery, further conquest became rare. Few emperors were inclined to trust a major command to a senator who might thus win glory and popularity with the soldiers, turning him into a rival. Even fewer emperors wanted to spend years on campaign conquering new lands.[4]

Although poets like Horace spoke with eager anticipation of the conquest of Britain – 'Augustus will be deemed a god, on earth when the Britons... have been added to our empire' – they were to be disappointed. There was a good deal of trade across the Channel, and some diplomatic activity, exiled British princes fleeing to the empire for sanctuary, but no new invasion. Augustus counted the tribes of the southeast as allies, who acknowledged Rome's supremacy and were thus part of the empire, even though they were not ruled directly – an attitude he extended to the great Parthian empire in the east and even the peoples of India. A little later the geographer Strabo declared that Britain was not worth conquering, for it posed no threat while the revenue from taxing the tribes was unlikely to cover the cost of the army needed to subdue the island.[5]

A Roman legionary from the time of the construction of Hadrian's Wall. He wears the famous banded armour (*lorica segmentata*) first reconstructed from finds at Corbridge.

Such concerns weighed less with the Emperor Claudius than his need for military glory. In the chaos after the assassination of his nephew Caligula in AD 41, praetorian guardsmen discovered Claudius hiding behind a curtain in the imperial palace. As the well-paid and pampered household troops of the emperor, they needed an emperor – any emperor – so proclaimed him because he was the only adult male member of Augustus's family available. There were few other grounds for his selection, but the Senate was forced to accept him because they could not defy the armed strength of the praetorians. Claudius was fifty-one, stammered, drooled and limped, and could boast of little public service and no military achievements.

In AD 43 he decided to make up for this and gathered four legions out of the twenty-eight then in service, reinforcing them with auxiliaries, sailors and other troops, and invaded Britain. The first target was the great tribal confederation dominating the southeast. Claudius arrived in person to oversee the capture of their capital at Camulodunum (Colchester), although he stayed in Britain for less than two weeks. His victory was celebrated in lavish style, not least because he had completed a task begun by his ancestor, the great Julius Caesar.

The island the Romans called Britannia was home to many separate peoples divided into tribes. Conflict between tribes was common, and internal power struggles almost as frequent, and there was no sense that they all belonged to a common nation. When the Romans arrived many leaders chose to ally with the invaders, seeing them as less of a threat than their neighbours and traditional enemies. In AD 60 the province was devastated by a rebellion provoked by the mistreatment of just such an ally, Queen Boudica of the Iceni sacking the veteran colony established at Camulodunum, the flourishing commercial town of Londinium (London) and the tribal centre at Verulamium (St Albans). Some tribes joined the revolt, while others stayed loyal, and Boudica was defeated in battle and the rebellion suppressed with considerable savagery. This was followed by conciliation, and it is striking that Lowland Britain never again witnessed any revolt against Roman rule over the next three and a half centuries.

It took longer for the Romans to secure control over what would become Wales, and there were frequent campaigns here until the 70s AD and a strong military presence for some time after that. Simultaneously, northern England was overrun and garrisons established in the area where Hadrian's Wall would later be built. Recent dendrochronological analysis of timbers used to build the first Roman fort at Carlisle (Luguvallium) show that the trees were felled in AD 72 or 73. Cnaeus Julius Agricola, governor of Britain from AD 78–84, pushed ever further north, driving deep into Scotland, where he routed an army of Caledonian tribesmen at Mons Graupius (the location of which is unknown). Permanent occupation was planned, and a network of forts was built, most notably the fortress at Inchtuthil in Perthshire, intended to house an entire legion.

Military crises in Germany and on the Danube then shifted the Emperor Domitian's attention away from Britain. One of the four legions and probably many auxiliaries were posted away from the province, and this substantial reduction in troop numbers prompted withdrawal from all bases north of the line between the estuaries of the rivers Forth and Clyde (and close to the area where the modern cities of Edinburgh and Glasgow now stand). Coin evidence suggests that this occurred around AD 86–87. At Inchtuthil a few of the internal buildings had not even been started before the base was evacuated, the defences slighted and the buildings demolished. The abandonment of these garrisons appears to have been ordered and not caused by hostile action, and the withdrawal may have been phased over a few years, with the line of towers and outposts along the Gask Ridge occupied a little longer before it too was decommissioned.

Very little is known about Britain during the reign of the Emperor Trajan (AD 98–117). Sites that would be closely associated with the Wall, such as Corbridge (Coria), Vindolanda, Carvoran, and Carlisle were garrisoned, and fascinating glimpses of life in the garrisons are supplied by the writing tablets found at Carlisle and especially at Vindolanda. Early in the second century AD, small outposts or fortlets were constructed in this area, notably the sites at Haltwhistle Burn and Throp, and perhaps some towers for observation or signalling. Around AD 106, the most northerly base left in Scotland, the fort at Newstead (Trimontium), was abandoned, as were other outposts. A properly laid-out, stone-paved and drained Roman road – known from its medieval name as the Stanegate because we do not know what the Romans called

This wooden writing tablet from Vindolanda invites the wife of the garrison commander to attend a friend's birthday party. This is the earliest-surviving handwriting by a woman in Britain, and probably in all of Europe.

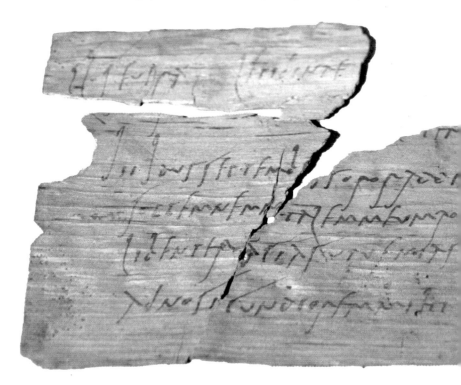

any of the roads they made in Britain – was constructed, running at least from Corbridge to Carlisle, each of which lay on major north–south roads. It ran a little to the south of where the Wall would be built, following the natural and easiest route between the Tyne and Eden valleys. At some point there was another drastic reduction in the size of the army of the province, when Legio IX (or often on inscriptions in the old-fashioned form as VIIII) Hispana was withdrawn, leaving just two legions in garrison, II Augusta and XX Valeria Victrix.

Trajan was one of the last great conquerors, adding Dacia (modern Romania) to the empire and in the last years of his life invading Parthia. Britain does not appear to have figured highly on his list of priorities and its governors had to do their job with substantially reduced military resources. Overstretch is the most likely reason for the withdrawal to the Tyne–Solway line in these years, and the concentration of a number of garrisons in this area effectively created a rough frontier line. In the years that followed

this was enhanced by the addition of outposts and the Stanegate road itself. There is little evidence for activity or any extension of the road to the east of Corbridge, and the focus of the army's ntion appears to have been the central and western sectors, facing the peoples known as the Novantae and Selgovae.

It is impossible to say how peaceful northern Britain was during Trajan's reign, but the presence of the bases along the Stanegate suggests that there was a real or perceived threat to Roman control and dominance in these areas. The strength report of a unit based at Vindolanda in the 90s AD includes six wounded men (*volnerati*) unfit for duty. While it is possible that they had been injured in an accident, this may hint at fighting, whether some small skirmish or a larger engagement. Another fragmentary writing tablet talks about the fighting styles of the local tribes: 'The Britons are unprotected by armour. There are very many cavalry. The cavalry do not use swords nor do the *Brittunculi* mount [or halt?] to throw javelins.' There is also a tombstone, later reused in the third-century bath-house at Vindolanda, commemorating the centurion Titus Annius, killed in the war (*interfectus in bello*). This probably dates to Trajan's reign, suggesting a reasonably large-scale conflict at some point to justify the use of the word 'war'. One fourth-century source claims that there were problems in Britain early in Hadrian's reign, making it possible that trouble had broken out in the last years of his predecessor. All in all, and given Hadrian's actions and subsequent history, it seems wise to assume that the frontier area posed an ongoing problem to the Roman administration, for all the dismissive talk of *Brittunculi* or 'little Britons'.[6]

At Mons Graupius the Caledonians had mustered an army claimed by our Roman source to number well over 30,000 warriors. The noblemen came to battle in agile, fast-moving chariots, each pulled by a pair of ponies. Julius Caesar had expressed his wonder when he encountered similar vehicles in 55

BC, for they had fallen out of use in Continental Europe at least a century previously. Used for skirmishing and as a stylish and impressive way of travelling to and from a fight, the noble warrior would spring down to fight on foot. Caesar said that the chariots were closely supported by groups of cavalry, although the latter are not mentioned in the single account of Mons Graupius. The bulk of the Caledonians were unarmoured infantrymen, wielding blunt-tipped slashing swords, their only protection a small shield. A sculpture from the Antonine Wall depicts a Roman cavalryman riding down three warriors very much like these, carrying little rectangular bucklers and long swords, although it is notable that the text from Vindolanda expressly states that the local horsemen did not carry swords. No doubt there was considerable variation between different communities and over the centuries.

The peoples of the north never formed a permanent professional army in any way resembling the Roman army. Few men were full-time warriors in the sense that fighting and training to fight was their main role in life. Such men would have been the chieftains and their armed followers. Among other Iron Age peoples in Gaul and elsewhere we hear that a leader's power was displayed by the number of warriors he kept in his household. The chiefs and such household warriors were likely to have the best equipment. These were men who rode in chariots, possessed good swords, perhaps mail armour or a helmet, and had the opportunity to train for war. In a small raid, the bulk or all of a force might consist of such well-equipped and highly motivated warriors, but in any larger army these would be a small minority among the mass of ordinary tribesmen. Less well equipped, such men might be brave and have some familiarity with weapons, especially if violence and theft between and within tribes was common. However, they would not be disciplined or used to obeying the orders of their leaders. As a general rule, the larger the tribal army was, the more clumsily it moved and manoeuvred, giving the Romans even more of an advantage in larger-scale warfare.[7]

Raiding to seize cattle or captives, and perhaps also trophies as proof of manhood and prowess, was the commonest form of military activity in the ancient world, and it is unlikely that northern Britain was an exception. The willingness and ability to plunder your neighbours, or their open submission to avoid such attacks, demonstrated to the wider world the strength of a leader or people. Caesar tells us of Germanic tribes who kept a depopulated strip of land around their borders as a warning to outsiders. This lower-level violence was probably the most common problem faced by the Roman army, whether it was directed against the Romans or their allies. The response over much of the empire was to assert dominance by proving that the empire and its army had a far greater capacity for violence than its enemies. The much-vaunted Roman peace was based on Roman victory and strength, not the product of peaceful co-existence. While such methods might intimidate, they also left a bitter legacy of hatred among the survivors of displays of Roman might, sowing the seeds for future conflict.

Northern Britain showing the lines of Hadrian's Wall, the Antonine Wall and earlier frontier deployments such as the towers and other installations along the Gask Ridge. Tribal names are based on Greco-Roman sources and the areas shown are approximate at best.

CALEDONIAN
TRIBES

Inchtuthil

Ardoch

Carpow

ANTONINE WALL

Inveresk

DUMNONII

VOTADINI

Newstead

Loudoun Hill

SELGOVAE

HADRIANS WALL

Vindolanda

South Shields

Corbridge

Carlisle

LOPOCARES

CARVETII

TEXTOVERDI

Moresby

Brougham

BRIGANTES

Piercebridge

GABRANTOVICES

Ravenglass

Aldborough

PARISI

York

SETANTI

Brough-on-Humber

Hadrian:
the man, the
emperor and
the grand design

In August 117, the ailing Trajan died in Cilicia. He was on his way back to Rome, his great eastern adventure having turned sour amid rebellions in the newly conquered territory and a simultaneous revolt of the Jewish population in Egypt, Cyprus and Cyrenaica. Hadrian was the son of the emperor's cousin, like him from Italica in Spain. His Latin was tinged with a provincial accent, but from his youth he had adored all things Greek, earning himself the nickname Graeculus or 'little Greek'. As an adult he sported a neater version of a philosopher's beard. He was forty-one, a clever man, albeit far too keen to show off his cleverness, and the closest male relative of the childless emperor. Rumour said that he had seduced the wives of other senators so that he could learn about their plans and so ease his rise to favour at the imperial court, but it was clear that the greatest passions in his life revolved around teenage boys.

Trajan had shown Hadrian some favour, but stopped a good way short of marking him out as his heir. The emperor's widow claimed that on his deathbed her husband had at long last adopted Hadrian and named him as his successor. Not everyone was convinced, and the rapid execution of four prominent senators back in Rome fuelled suspicion, even though it deterred any open opposition. Hadrian was never truly popular with the Senate from then on, even though he was far from being a tyrant. Tact was not his strong point, and he lacked the ability to win affection from the nobility. For years the emperor openly paraded his lover, the Bithynian youth Antinous, declaring the lad to be a god after he drowned in the Nile in somewhat mysterious circumstances. Affairs of this sort were supposed to be discreet, not exuberantly public, and it only added to the secret resentment felt by most aristocrats. Hadrian does not appear to have cared much about the feelings of others. He spent lavishly on a major remodelling of Athens, but crowned his achievement with an arch bearing the inscription:

This bronze head from a larger than life sized statue of the Emperor Hadrian was found in the River Thames. Hadrian came to Britain in AD 122, and was only the second emperor to visit the island as emperor.

'This is the city of Hadrian, not of Theseus [the city's mythical founder].'

Insecure, given the doubts over his right to rule, and unpopular, Hadrian had no desire to spend years regaining and securing territory in the east, and most of Trajan's recent conquests were abandoned. There were to be no wars of expansion under Hadrian, but it was vital to retain the loyalty of the army and to demonstrate Rome's continued military dominance, and he spent much of his reign touring the provinces and visiting the legions, watching them at drill, praising and rewarding. No emperor since Augustus had travelled as much as Hadrian would during his reign, visiting almost every part of the empire. Such travel could be arduous, and he was praised for his endurance as well as the personal example he set, leading soldiers on route marches and eating the same rations issued to them. Hadrian had a mind for detail, and if he chose not to lead his soldiers in war, he was keen to show a deep interest in their lives, imposing strict discipline, but moderating it with fair treatment and generous rewards for talented officers and men.[8]

In Britain Hadrian was faced with an outbreak of warfare, possibly inherited from his predecessor. An experienced governor from the Danube frontier was sent to take charge and achieved victory within a few years. In 122 another proven commander, Aulus Platorius Nepos, took over, arriving by 17 July – one of those rare precise dates, in this case derived from a document issued to a discharged soldier. At some point during the same year, Hadrian came to Britain in person, staying for a few months. Around the same time, the provincial garrison was increased in size by the addition of a third legion, VI Victrix. Hadrian's personal involvement in the decision to construct the Wall and in its design is clear. It is generally assumed that he gave the order after visiting the area, so that the surveying and construction began no earlier than 122. However, we know little about Roman planning methods and imperial decision-making, and cannot be sure that the project was not devised – and perhaps even begun – earlier than this, so that the visiting emperor could come and inspect progress. Timber used to construct a stockade along a section of the frontier in Germany was felled two years before Hadrian visited the region in 121, so a similar advance order is possible in Britain.

The initial design for Hadrian's Wall was grand, if not as grand as it would become, and this is an indication of the emperor's personal involvement. Hadrian was obsessed with architecture and loved designing great buildings, a passion reflected in his rebuilding of the Pantheon in Rome, with its spectacular domed roof, and in his sprawling villa complex at Tivoli. The Wall was more functional, but made up for this in sheer size.

The western section for 31 Roman miles (46 km) from Bowness-on-Solway was built of turf, timber and earth, with a rampart some 20 feet (6 m) wide at its base. The line was then continued by a stone wall for 49 Roman miles (73 km) to the east, eventually ending at Wallsend on the Tyne. This wall was planned to be about 10 feet (3 m) wide and was freestanding, unlike the stone walls sometimes used in forts which were backed by an earth bank. Every Roman mile there was to be a milecastle – a small fortlet, its north wall part of the Wall itself, and both north and south walls having a gateway. Between the milecastles and also forming part of the Wall itself were two turrets, which were built in stone, even on the turf wall. Throughout its length the Wall was fronted by a wide and deep ditch, except where nature provided an even more formidable protection in the form of a cliff. Beyond Bowness-on-Solway, following the coastline of Cumbria, the pattern of stone turrets and turf and timber fortlets continued for about 20 miles (32 km), but in this case there was no continuous wall or ditch.

The surveyors marking out the line of the Wall appear to have begun near the coasts and worked inland. Construction work was undertaken by detachments drawn from the three legions, and there are hints of slight variations in the templates used by each one, even though we cannot allocate them to specific units. The Wall was not built section by section, completing everything before moving on to the next piece. Instead, parties started to build at locations all along the line, sometimes laying down no more than foundations and perhaps a few courses of stone, and elsewhere completing work, especially on turrets and milecastles.

The turf wall is likely to have been completed first, for the methods involved were faster and familiar to all the soldiers – most army bases were made using the same methods. It also seems that priority was given to the curtain wall in the sector running through the gentler country on the eastern side, especially from Wall miles 7–22. In the rugged central section there was more concern to build turrets, and probably the northern wall of milecastles which most likely had a tower over the gateway. This suggests a line of raised sentry stations, each capable of signalling back to a fort on the Stanegate just to the south. Milecastles near the routes along the river valleys cutting through the planned line of the Wall also came early in the schedule, guarding country readily infiltrated by raiders. Many turrets and milecastles were built with short sections of curtain wall butting on to them, making it easier to bond with the main wall when it was finally joined to them.

Major changes to the design of the Wall were then made, either by Hadrian in person if his visit was to inspect a project already underway, or after consultation with him if it was only begun in 122. In the original design only the small detachments of troops in milecastles and turrets garrisoned the Wall itself, and substantial numbers were stationed a mile or two to the rear in the forts on the Stanegate. As we have seen, as yet there is no

Reconstruction of a section of part of a milecastle from the Turf Wall on display at Vindolanda. In the original design, the western section of Hadrian's Wall was built in turf and timber.

good evidence for garrisons behind the eastern section of the Wall, but it is usually assumed that these existed or were planned on a similar scale to the bases on the Stanegate in the central and western sections. Whether or not this is correct, a decision was then made that the number of troops serving near the Wall was to be drastically increased by the addition of forts actually on the curtain walls each designed to hold a complete auxiliary unit.

As with the whole project, the new forts were not all constructed at the same time, and, again as with the wider project, over the course of time there were changes made to their specific design. At first, the new forts were laid out so that they projected well to the north of the Wall, with three out of the four main fort gateways beyond it, increasing the number of crossings giving access to the north. Presumably this was judged to be excessive, and forts built later in the sequence lie behind the curtain, forming their northern wall and having only one grand double-gateway leading through the Wall to give access to the

north. Eventually there were fifteen forts on the Wall, each about 7–7.5 miles (11–12 km) apart, with at least three more on the line of the Stanegate continuing in full use for most of the life of the Wall.

There are hints at interruptions in the building schedule, perhaps of changing priorities. Some sections of foundation or low walls appear to have been left open to the weather for one or more seasons before building resumed. It was difficult to build a freestanding wall much higher than about 5 feet (1.5 m) without employing scaffolding, and the timber needed to make this for so vast a project is likely to have been the biggest restriction on its progress. Much of this region, especially on the coastal plains, had been cleared of forest in the pre-Roman Iron Age by local farmers, so that less wood was readily available. Long stretches of the Wall were built over ploughed fields, the marks of the ploughing still there beneath the earliest layers of Roman occupation.

At Housesteads and Chesters construction of the forts required the demolition of turrets which had already been completed and which show signs of occupation. In other cases forts lay on top of planned or even completed milecastles. Excavations at Birdoswald have shown that the rampart of the turf wall was used to fill in the ditch so that the fort could be built over it. In this case the site was wooded, making it the exception to the general pattern of construction over cleared farmland. The timber felled to clear the site was immediately used in construction of the fort. Like milecastles, forts were built in the same material as each sector of curtain wall, so were in turf and timber in the west and stone in the east. The only exception to this was that in early phases of the stone forts some internal buildings were timber.

Another change made soon after the decision to add forts was a reduction in the width of the Wall itself to around 7 feet 6 inches (2.3 m) wide. Scholars term this the Narrow Wall, as opposed to the Broad Wall. It is unclear how much Broad Wall was ever completed to full height, and the decision to reduce the gauge of the curtain greatly reduced the time and material needed in construction. Some milecastles were wholly or partly built to Broad Wall widths, while others were wholly Narrow Wall, providing evidence for the order in which they were constructed.

After the fort decision was taken, although before all were planned and constructed, another feature was added behind almost the entire length of the Wall. This is known as the Vallum, because in the eighth century Bede mistook it for an earlier earth wall. Its principal feature is a ditch, so the name ought to be Fossa, but Vallum has stuck and is still used by scholars. The ditch was about 20 feet (6 m) wide, with sloping sides so that its flat bottom was somewhat narrower. Spoil from the ditch was raised into a 20-foot (6-m) wide mound on either side, set back some 30 feet (9 m) from the edges. The width of all its elements appears to match a Roman measurement known as an *actus* of 120 Roman feet (*c*.35.5 m). For much of its length the Vallum ran close to the Wall, widening to allow room for milecastles and forts, but in the central section it stays on the lower ground rather than climbing the crags so that the interval between the Wall and the Vallum is wider. There were causeways across the Vallum for each fort and a handful are known to have been added to permit access from certain milecastles through the north mound. The north–south Roman road known today as Dere Street after its Anglo-Saxon name (and providing the foundations for the modern A68) was provided with both a crossing over the Vallum and its own gateway through the Wall to the west of milecastle 22, and similar provision is assumed for the other major north–south road running via Carlisle.

As ever, the precise sequence of decisions and construction can only be guessed at. At some point later in Hadrian's reign, the stretch of turf wall for several miles to the west of the River

Irthing near Birdoswald was replaced in stone, as was the fort itself. There may have been a substantial pause in construction, and similar halts occurred elsewhere, if not necessarily at the same time. There is evidence for heavy fighting under Hadrian, apart from the war at the start of his reign, and various dates have been suggested for this, notably $c.123-4$ or later in the decade. The need to draw troops away for active campaigning is an attractive explanation for such lulls in building work, as is the idea that the Romans' new fortification and stronger military presence provoked hostility in the people of the area, but there could be other explanations as well, for the army was given many tasks and had limited manpower. The extension of the observation system to the Cumbrian coast does suggest a real threat, presumably of raiders coming by boat.

We shall examine each element of the system in more detail, but it is worth noting that in its original and modified designs, Hadrian's Wall was a formidable obstacle to unauthorized movement. It was not meant to hinder the Roman army, who controlled its numerous crossing points. Compared to other frontiers the system is on a far grander scale. The line Hadrian ordered built in Germany was a simple stockade fence with a ditch behind it – an obstacle to slow down anyone trying to cross it, but nothing more.

One of the many steep slopes climbed by Hadrian's Wall, especially in its central section.

Building and
Manning the Wall:
legions and *auxilia*

The Roman army was based around the legions recruited from Roman citizens. There were thirty of these when the Wall was built, so that the garrison of Britain represented one tenth of the entire legionary strength of the empire. Each legion had a theoretical strength of around 5,000 men, almost all of whom were heavily armed infantrymen. These were organized into ten cohorts, each consisting of six centuries of eighty men who were commanded by a centurion. (The First Cohort was different, having five double-strength centuries and the task of guarding the precious eagle standard of the legion.)

The legions were supported by the *auxilia*, men recruited from the provinces who gained citizenship only at the end of their military service. The *auxilia* included both infantry and cavalry as well as specialized troops such as archers. They were not divided into legion-sized formations, but formed in independent units similar in size to a legionary cohort. There were infantry cohorts of 480 or 800 men, mixed cohorts (*cohortes equitatae*) of 480 infantry and 120 horsemen or 800 infantry and 240 horsemen, and cavalry *alae* of 512 or 768 respectively. The theoretical organization of the various types of army unit in the second and early third centuries is given in the table below:

UNIT TYPE	FOOT	CENTURIES	HORSE	TURMAE
Cohors quingenaria	480	6 each of 80 men led by a centurion		
Cohors quingenaria equitata	480	6 each of 80 men led by a centurion	120	4 each of 30 men led by a decurion
Cohors milliaria	800	10 each of 80 men led by a centurion		
Cohors milliaria equitata	800	10 each of 80 men led by a centurion	240	8 each of 30 men led by a decurion
Ala quingenaria			512	16 each of 32 men led by a decurion
Ala milliaria			768	24 each of 32 men led by a decurion
Second to Tenth Cohorts of a legion			480	6 each of 80 men led by a centurion
First Cohort of a legion			800	5 each of 160 led by a centurion

From Augustus onwards there were at least as many auxiliaries as legionaries, and by the second century AD there were significantly more. Overall, the garrison of Britain probably had a theoretical strength of more than 35,000 men, making it larger than the army in almost every other province. It was commanded by the provincial governor (*legatus augusti*), a senator, usually at least in his forties and who had already held command in a less prestigious military province.

Although they were Roman citizens, only a tiny minority of legionaries came from Italy, and most were from the substantial communities of citizens living in Gaul, Spain, North Africa and other provinces. Auxiliaries were organized into units with ethnic names, for instance Spaniards, Gauls, Dacians, Thracians, Hamians from Syria and Batavians and Tungrians from the Rhineland. When first raised such units were recruited from these peoples. Over time, especially when posted far from their homeland, it is clear that men from other races enlisted and served. The language of command and administration in all units was Latin, although Hadrian encouraged regiments to keep ethnic war-cries. Britons served in distinct units, but were also present in many other cohorts and *alae* stationed on the Wall.

Some units had simple titles, such as *cohors II Delmatarum eq.* or 'second part-mounted regiment of Delmatae', which was recruited from modern-day Croatia and served at Carvoran in the third century, or *cohors I Hamiorum sagittariourum* or 'first regiment of Hamian archers' which had been at the same fort under Hadrian, then on the Antonine Wall and then back at Carvoran under Marcus Aurelius. A few units acquired additional titles as rewards for valour or loyalty. Thus there was the *ala Augusta ob virtutem appellata*, the 'cavalry regiment called Augustan on account of its valour' and the even more elaborately named *ala Augusta Gallorum Petriana Milliaria civium Romanorum* or 'double-strength cavalry regiment of Gauls, originally raised

by Petrianus, the emperor's own, of Roman citizens'. Granting citizenship to an entire regiment of soldiers was a rare reward for conspicuous service. The grant applied only to soldiers currently serving with the unit, but the title was kept permanently, even when all the men who had been made citizens had served their time and been discharged from the army.

In the second century AD most recruits were volunteers, with only occasional periods of conscription, often when auxiliary units were raised as part of a treaty with a tribe or when a major war occurred. All had to be freeborn, for the army was not supposed to be a refuge for runaway slaves. Army pay was little different to the wages of a farm labourer, but it was regular, and soldiers were fed, clothed, and provided with better medical care than the poor in civilian life. Literate recruits stood a good chance of promotion, which brought better pay and conditions. All this was set against extremely harsh discipline and a minimum enlistment of twenty-five years. Even the food and clothes issued to soldiers came at a price deducted from their pay.

Officers were drawn from higher up the social scale than the men they commanded, and the most senior were invariably citizens of considerable status. In charge of each legion was a legate (*legatus legionis*) who was a senator, usually in his early thirties, supported by a senior tribune in his late teens who was just starting a senatorial career. Equestrians or 'knights' (*equites*), the next social class below senators, provided the bulk of the army's senior officers. Typically such men first commanded an auxiliary cohort, then became one of five junior tribunes in each legion, before receiving the command of a cavalry *ala*. The officer commanding an auxiliary cohort or *ala* was called a prefect (*praefectus*), except in the case of some more prestigious units, where his title was tribune.

Senators were obliged to own land in Italy, although many, like Hadrian, had grown up in the provinces. Equestrians came

This Roman auxiliary infantryman is typical of the soldiers who manned Hadrian's Wall in the second and early third centuries.

overleaf: Northern Gateway of milecastle 37, showing the third century alteration to leave only a narrow doorway.

from all over the empire and were men of considerable property and education. A few chose to serve instead as legionary centurions, but most centurions in the legions and the auxilia lacked equestrian status. Even so, they had to be highly literate, and many appear to have come from the minor gentry of Italy and the provinces, serving all or most of their time in the army as centurions. Centurion was not a specific rank, but a grade of officer, whose responsibilities, pay and status varied considerably. Much less is known about the background and careers of auxiliary as opposed to legionary centurions.

The Roman army was very much the army of the empire, recruited from the provinces and led by men from the imperial elite. Soldiers usually served their entire twenty-five years with the same unit, and increasingly often that unit remained in the same province for generation after generation. In contrast, senatorial and equestrian officers moved from posting to posting around the empire, and many legionary centurions also served in a succession of different units in different provinces. This meant that northern Britain, like any frontier zone, drew men from far afield to serve there, the more senior usually only for short tours. In the second century AD, a significant minority of the Senate's 600 members had been to Britain, and many had been to the north. Although on the edge of the empire, the sheer size of the provincial garrison meant that Britain was always important, its governorship a rare honour reserved only for the most distinguished and loyal senators.

*

Hadrian's Wall was built by legionaries, the work being divided up and allocated to sub-units who then commemorated what they had done in simple inscriptions. 'From the fifth cohort the century of Caecilius Proculus built this' (*coh[ortis] V c[enturia] Caecili Procul[i]*) or 'The Sixth Legion built this' (*leg[io] VI*

V[ictrix]). Every legion included a large number of specialists and craftsmen, while other soldiers provided more or less skilled labour. An inscription from the Vallum recording work done by an auxiliary cohort suggests that this huge but simpler task was allocated to these soldiers, whose units generally contained a much lower proportion of specialists. In later years, auxiliaries would undertake more complex building projects, especially in the forts.[9]

The Wall itself was a simple structure, and the reliance on legionaries to build it has more to do with these bigger units being easier to organize on a large scale than auxiliary units a tenth of the size. Stone was quarried from the nearest available source, usually less than 2 miles (3 km) from the site. Squared rubble – the term used by stonemasons for stones more or less roughly squared off rather than precisely worked – was used for the two facing walls, with a core of smaller stones bonded with clay. It was not particularly well made by Roman standards, the priority being to complete this immense stone wall as quickly as possible. Some of the stone used was of very poor quality, so that in patches it was barely squared off at all.

More care was given to the important features, such as turrets and buildings, and especially the gateways in forts and milecastles. These required considerably more skill than building the wall itself, which suggests that all the best craftsmen and teams were assigned to these tasks, leaving the bulk of other work to be performed by the less skilled legionaries and supervising engineers. Interruptions in the process may well have meant that one team laid foundations before moving on, with another or even several other parties completing successive stages of the building. There is clear evidence of haste in the last phase of construction, so that standards of work became lower in the hurry to finish things off. The gateways at Housesteads, Chesters, and the stone fort that replaced the timber one at Birdoswald,

overleaf: The stone steps in milecastle 48 (Poltross Burn) are the only ones to survive anywhere on Hadrian's Wall.

all made use of cruder, less finished stone in the upper courses. At milecastle 37 subsidence caused a crack next to the northern gate which was made good, but was still visible in the twentieth century when archaeologists temporarily cleared away stonework from a later period. Hadrian's Wall in its early phases presents a strange mixture of grandiose imperial project alongside haste and corner-cutting by the men tasked with turning this concept into reality. Yet whether in design or implementation, the willingness to adapt shows a desire to make the whole system work.

In the end, its effectiveness would depend on the troops stationed on and around the Wall. As far as we can tell, every fort on the Wall was designed to house an entire auxiliary cohort or *ala*, rather than a mixed force drawn from detachments of several units. For much of the time the picture may well have been less neat, with parts of the garrison posted away and other troops passing through and living in a fort for short or long periods, but it does show an expectation that in normal circumstances each sector would be controlled by a distinct auxiliary unit. Thus even though legionaries had built the Wall, it would be manned primarily by auxiliaries.

Building work continued throughout Hadrian's reign until his death in 138 (it was claimed that he was such a skilled astrologer that he was able to predict the day and time with precision). His successor was his adopted son, Antoninus Pius, who insisted that the Senate deify his 'father' in spite of its reluctance to do so. Deification was the normal honour voted to a good emperor on his death, and most senators were keen to show their dislike of Hadrian now that he was dead and unable to strike back. Realization that his successor was keen for the honour to be awarded soon persuaded them of the advantages of pleasing the new emperor. Unlike Hadrian, Antoninus Pius enjoyed the security of knowing that his claim to the imperial throne was unimpeachable, but he was also a very different character to his predecessor, having a mild nature and lacking both energy and passion. During his reign no senator was executed, and his popularity never waned. Unlike Hadrian, Antoninus Pius spent his entire reign in Italy. Yet although he never saw Britain or its northern frontier, he had very different plans for his army there.

Fresh minds: Antoninus Pius to Septimius Severus

War appears to have erupted in Britain early in the new emperor's reign. The Greek writer Pausanias says that 'the Brigantes... had begun a war, invading Gerunia, which is subject to the Romans'. The Brigantes were a large tribe occupying much of what would become northern England. Most lived south of the Wall, although it is quite possible that it had cut through tribal territory, so that some Brigantes or closely related peoples now lived north of the Roman military zone. On the other hand, the name was often applied loosely by the Greeks and Romans to Britons in general, and perhaps especially the northern tribes. The district Pausanias calls Gerunia is unknown, and the name may be garbled, while some scholars prefer to believe that the passage talks of troubles in Raetia on the continent rather than Britain. Yet disturbances in Britain, most probably well to the north of Hadrian's Wall, make most sense of what happened, and perhaps tribes allied to Rome were attacked by neighbours.[10]

The result was a major change in Roman deployment. Hadrian's Wall ceased to be the main part of the provincial frontier, and instead the army advanced into Lowland Scotland, and constructed the Antonine Wall on the line between the Forth and Clyde. The new wall was built in turf and timber; forts formed part of it from the start, but unlike on Hadrian's Wall not all were designed to house a complete *ala* or cohort. Instead they were bases for composite groups mixing infantry and cavalry and troops from two or more separate units. There were also fortlets similar to milecastles along the rampart, but a line of turrets was not part of the system and was presumably seen as unnecessary. Like Hadrian's Wall, there were outposts beyond the line of the wall itself. Antoninus Pius was acclaimed as *imperator* or 'victorious general' by the Senate for a victory in Britain, the only time during his reign that he accepted this title.

The move stripped Hadrian's Wall of its main function and it was decommissioned. Gates from milecastles were removed and the pivot stones in which they had been mounted were smashed, so that anyone could pass through. At the same time earth was taken from the mounds on either side of the Vallum to help make causeways across it, at intervals of 135 feet (41 m) or so along much of the line, although in some areas these were never completed or even started. It is possible that a handful of the forts on Hadrian's Wall continued to be manned, albeit probably by substantially reduced garrisons. The rest were abandoned or maintained by very small numbers of personnel as holding units.

Antoninus Pius died in 161 and was succeeded by his adopted son, Marcus Aurelius, an earnest man and a philosopher, whose *Meditations* survive. It is a deeply personal book, made all the more fascinating because it was written by the ruler of most of the known world and deals with his struggle to live a good life, to rule well and not to be corrupted by power struggles or too upset by criticism: 'it is the king's part to do good and be ill spoke of'. Death is a constant theme. Marcus Aurelius had a dozen children, most of whom died in infancy, and his sorrow preoccupied him, as did the prospect of his own end: 'in a short while you will be no one and nowhere, as are Hadrian and Augustus'. Hadrian is mentioned elsewhere in the book, but this was not a work dealing with the details of government and events. Although some of the *Meditations* was written during the long and brutal campaigns Marcus Aurelius waged on the Danube, these conflicts are not discussed.[11]

The same is true of the trouble that had broken out again in Britain early in his reign. This led to another change of policy and around about this time the Antonine Wall was abandoned and Hadrian's Wall once again became the main feature in the frontier. The transition was carefully managed and prepared, rather than being the result of disaster or panicked retreat, for excavation of sites on the Antonine Wall reveal deliberate demolition rather than violent destruction. An inscription records building work

overleaf: Reconstruction painting of Housesteads fort in the early third century. This painting of the fort in the third century AD should be compared to the aerial photograph of the site today (see pages 14–15).

at one of the forts on Hadrian's Wall and also on the Wall itself in 158, while in the same year the abandoned outpost fort at Birrens was rebuilt. This was just the start of substantial restoration and remodelling of the Wall. Gates were replaced in milecastles, and the remaining stretch of turf wall was rebuilt in stone, which makes it clear that the original decision under Hadrian to build it in turf was not simply through lack of suitable stone close to the line of the Wall. A smaller mound – known as the marginal mound – on the south side of the Vallum ditch may date to this period, blocking off the causeways so that it once again became an effective obstacle. Refinements continued for decades. One of the biggest changes was the construction of the Military Way, a road running between the Wall and Vallum, connecting milecastles and turrets as well as the forts. In the original design a footpath had crossed the rivers. Now these were bridged to take the road across these obstacles.

In 180 Marcus Aurelius died and was succeeded by his eighteen-year-old son Commodus, the only one of his sons to survive him. Unlike his father in almost every way, the new emperor soon rejected the dull routine of administration and the hardships of supervising the army on campaign. Instead he preferred to return to Rome, spending most of his twelve-year reign in and around the great city. The senator Cassius Dio, who knew both father and son, described Commodus as 'not naturally evil, but simple minded'. He and other senators were appalled by Commodus's growing obsession with the circus games and gladiators. The young emperor was fond of showing off his skill with a bow by shooting down from the imperial box in the Colosseum and slaughtering animals in the arena. On other occasions he fought display bouts as a gladiator, his opponents armed with blunt weapons to make sure that no accidental injury was inflicted on the emperor.

Yet for all his antics, in the early years of Commodus's reign problems in the provinces were dealt with competently by his subordinates. A Byzantine epitome of Dio's text – the full version is lost – also tells us that 'the tribes in that island [of Britain], crossing the wall that separated them from the Roman legions, proceeded to do much mischief and cut down a general together with his troops'. The experienced Ulpius Marcellus was given charge of the province and 'ruthlessly put down the barbarians of Britain'. Coins commemorating a victory in Britain were issued in 184. These days archaeologists are reluctant to interpret burnt layers on a site as the mark of violent destruction. This is a healthy reaction against earlier scholars who were inclined to assume fires were deliberate rather than accidental, and who were over fond of tying the remains as closely as possible to any event mentioned in our literary sources. Yet the pendulum may have swung too far the other way, and recently one scholar has argued that work at Corbridge and Halton Chesters (the closest fort on the Wall to Dere Street) does suggest a layer of burning on each site dating to around the 180s that was probably deliberate, making it quite possible that they attest to the destruction caused by this war.[12]

Dio does not say whether the commander killed by the invaders was a legionary legate commanding one of the legions in Britain or the provincial governor, the *legatus augusti* himself in charge of the whole province. Ulpius Marcellus is attested as legate of Britain in 178 on a document recording the honourable discharge and grant of citizenship to auxiliary soldiers, which means that he arrived to govern Britain under Marcus Aurelius, so he was not sent by Commodus. This has led to the suggestion that it was his successor as *legatus augusti* who died in the fighting or was recalled for his failure, and that Marcellus was sent back to the province and served a second spell as governor – something very rare, but not impossible. On the other hand, if the officer killed was a legionary legate, then Marcellus may already have been in the province rather than sent by Commodus to deal with the crisis. As usual, a brief description in one of our sources raises almost as many questions as it answers. We simply cannot say which peoples were involved in the war, why it broke out, or trace its course, in particular the circumstances in which the attackers overran the Wall.

Marcus Aurelius's reign had seen the start of the Antonine plague, an unidentified epidemic which was carried by troops returning from a successful invasion of Parthia and later spread throughout the empire. Cities and army bases were especially prone to outbreaks, since both brought large numbers of people into close contact. At the same time, there were arduous campaigns on the upper Danube. Both factors may well have depleted the garrisons in Britain, so that it was less able to dominate the northern frontier. Later in Commodus's reign, discontent among the troops in Britain led to mutiny on more than one occasion.[13]

Commodus was strangled in his bath on New Year's Eve 192. His successor lasted only a few months before he was murdered by the praetorian guard, who were angered when he failed to pay them all of a promised bounty. The civil war which followed was fought between the governors of the three biggest military provinces in the empire, Britain, Upper Pannonia on the Danube and Syria. The legate of Britain was Decimus Clodius Albinus, and he drew off a substantial part of the garrison along with troops from other provinces to mass the huge army which he led to defeat at Lugdunum (modern Lyons) in 197. The victor was Lucius Septimius Severus, a native of Lepcis Magna in North Africa, but a Roman senator just like the 'Spanish' Trajan and Hadrian.

Severus was a hard-nosed, ruthless politician who realized that he might easily face a challenge from another senator in charge of an army. Soon he named his infant sons as co-rulers, in an effort to show that the dynasty would survive whatever happened to him. He also declared himself the son of Marcus

Aurelius even though there was no basis for the claim. Although feared by senators, Severus was never popular and relied openly on force to maintain his power. He reinforced the already substantial total of guard units in Rome with a newly formed legion stationed a short distance away. During his reign he fought two major foreign wars, leading an expedition against the Parthians and then later against the Caledonians, and it was no coincidence that this gave him a chance to confirm the loyalty of the armies in Syria and Britain, both of which had fought for his enemies in the civil war.

That is not to say that either war was unnecessary. At some stage during the early years of Severus's reign there was trouble in the north of Britain, centring on a previously unknown group called the Maeatae, who may have lived near the River Forth and the line of the abandoned Antonine Wall. Breaking their old alliances with Rome, many of the Caledonian tribes joined them, and Severus's newly appointed governor judged them too strong to fight with the weak garrison of the province and 'was compelled to purchase peace from the Maeatae for a large sum', receiving some hostages as surety. Some of the hoards of silver *denarii* found in Scotland and dating to the turn of the second to third centuries AD may represent subsidies paid at this time to buy peace.[14]

The peace did not prove permanent. There was fighting in 207, and in 208 Severus came to Britain and spent the next three years campaigning in the north. He brought substantial reinforcements, including detachments (or 'vexillations', named after the flag or *vexillum* they carried) from a number of legions. Marching camps from Scotland associated with these campaigns are some of the largest known from Britain, and for a while bases were re-established beyond the Forth–Clyde line. The enemy proved elusive, avoiding pitched battle and instead fighting by ambush and raid, making the most of their knowledge of the country. Dio says that they used sheep and cattle as bait to lure the Roman soldiers into ambushes. Severus ordered brutal reprisals and eventually received the submission of the tribes, but a renewal of war prompted him to order even more savagery in the hope of terrifying the tribes into surrender. The emperor's health was poor, so that he had to be carried in a litter for much of the time, and the rigours of campaigning used up his last strength, for he died in York in 211. In spite of the advance to the far north, Septimius Severus's reign saw a good deal of work restoring and repairing Hadrian's Wall and there is no hint of any plan to abandon it in favour of a more northerly line.

Our literary sources are silent for most of the rest of the third century, so that it is impossible to say how long the tribes remained cowed by the emperor's demonstration of Roman might. Late in the century the name Picts is first attested for some of the peoples of Scotland. Most scholars assume that groups already living in the area came together under some loose confederation, a trend shared with other tribal societies living beyond the frontiers of the Roman empire. The name means 'the painted' – and as early as Julius Caesar's day Roman commentators talked of the Britons' fondness for tattooing and painting themselves – so it may simply be a slang term imposed by outsiders and may long pre-date its first appearance in our meagre sources. We simply do not have enough evidence to say whether or not the tribes of the north changed much in their social and political organization.

Yet for the Romans this was certainly an era of change. The dying Severus made his two sons joint successors, supposedly giving them the grim advice: 'love one another, indulge the soldiers, and despise everyone else'. Within a year the older brother had murdered his younger sibling. He was in turn killed in 217, stabbed to death by a centurion in his own bodyguard, and this was the start of generations of civil war unlike anything in Rome's past history. Long-term stability never really returned and the Western Roman empire faded into history with the deposition of its last emperor in 476. For much of the time Britain escaped the worst of the internal chaos, although it must have seen frequent troop withdrawals as soldiers were drawn off to back leaders in the long succession of civil wars.

Some of the power struggles lasted for many years, so that several rival emperors ruled simultaneously, each controlling only a part of the whole empire. For more than a decade from 260 a succession of emperors ruled an empire consisting of the Rhineland, Gaul, Britain and much of Spain. Scholars conventionally refer to this as the Gallic empire, but as far as they were concerned these men were the legitimate emperors of Rome, and it was simply that they were unwilling or unable to bring the other provinces under their sway. Eventually, weakened by the same sort of internal power struggles that ravaged the whole empire, the western provinces were brought back under the control of central authority by the emperor Aurelian. In 286 Carausius, a commander sent to deal with seaborne raiders in the English Channel, declared himself emperor, and once again Britain became part of a separate regime that still considered itself Roman in every important respect. At least one major attempt by the emperors controlling the rest of the empire to invade and reclaim the island was defeated, but in the end Carausius was murdered by a rival, who was in turn defeated by one of the emperors from the 'main' Roman empire. In both these periods, Britain was culturally and politically Roman; it was just that for a while there was more than one Roman empire. Inevitably this must have disrupted the army's system of administration, recruitment, promotion and supply, but our meagre evidence makes it impossible to trace this dislocation, and gives a false impression of continuity and stability.

By the early third century, most of the forts on Hadrian's Wall were garrisoned by units that would remain in place for

the remainder of Roman rule in Britain. This may mean no more than that their headquarters and records were based there and that maintaining this arrangement was seen as sensible. As always it is harder to say where the majority of the soldiers in each unit actually were at any time – and indeed how strong the unit was in practice and not simply in theory. Probably around the 230s the barrack blocks in several forts were reduced in size by roughly half, which does suggest that it was expected that fewer men would be present. This most likely reflects a reduction in the nominal strength of cohorts and *alae*. Other, less regular units appear at the same time at Housesteads and elsewhere, so that perhaps the smaller units were augmented by less formally

One of the third century 'chalet' barracks at Housesteads consisting of a row of separate huts. Unlike the earlier barracks, it was not a single range, but a row of individual huts or chalets.

trained warriors from other frontiers, but the result may still have been to reduce the total number of troops available in the area of the Wall.

At some time late in the second or early in the third century, many turrets on Hadrian's Wall were decommissioned and their entrances blocked up. They were subsequently demolished and not replaced. This was especially true in the central section, where only a few remained in use. It looks as if most or all of the smaller installations on the Cumbrian coast fell out of use some time before this, and limited excavation has shown no trace of reoccupation of towers and milefortlets after the return from the Antonine Wall. However, the forts along the coast continued in full use, which suggests that a significant military presence was still felt necessary in this area.

Around the time that the turrets on the Wall fell out of use, other changes were made. In many milecastles the northern gateway was walled up, sometimes leaving only a narrow doorway permitting access to the outside, sufficient for maintenance of the Wall. Wherever this occurred, the causeways across the ditch were removed or blocked. Yet in spite of these changes, the milecastles continued to be used by the army, and it is now time to look in more detail at the physical components of Hadrian's Wall as we try to understand how it was intended to function and how this developed over the years.

The Anatomy of
Hadrian's Wall

The northernmost element of the barrier was the ditch, which ran along most of the frontage of the Wall, with a few exceptions, usually where natural features rendered it either impractical or superfluous. More often than not it was V-shaped, some 9 feet (2.7 m) deep and 28 feet (8.5 m) wide. The spoil from the ditch was piled on the northern side and then smoothed into a gently sloping mound which effectively made the ditch deeper, but offered no cover to any attacker. Although in older studies diagrams of the ditch have a rectangular trench at the bottom, it is now clear that this was rare. In many respects it was similar to the ditches surrounding Roman forts. Causeways were provided in front of fort gateways, and in the original design appear to have been normal in front of milecastles. As we have seen, most of the latter were removed or blocked in the late second or early third century.

However, it should not surprise us that there was considerable variation over the course of an obstacle stretching some 80 Roman miles (120 km). Some parts of the ditch are more U-shaped than V-shaped. In sections where the ground sloped down away from the Wall, there are stretches where the mound was made steeper on the inside, creating a counterscarp in the language of the early modern fortification. Another device employed where the natural gradient was insufficient was to dig out a steeper inner side of the ditch, at times creating a one-sided ditch. Some of these alternative approaches provide a shallower trench, but all perform the same basic function. The ditch was intended to slow down anyone trying to get across the Wall from the north, while keeping them in plain sight of the defenders. Variations in its design appear most common in the craggy central sector of the Wall. Famously, at Limestone Corner near milecastle 30 the party digging the ditch left a number of granite boulders in place. Marks from their tools as they tried to drive wedges into the stone and break the pieces up can still be seen today, for at no point in the following centuries did anyone bother to complete the work.

Between the inner edge of the ditch and the Wall itself is a flat patch of ground known as the berm – once again a term lifted from siege warfare in the age of cannon, but it is convenient to use since we do not know what the Romans called this feature. In the stone wall it is usually some 20 feet (6 m) wide, whereas on the turf wall it was narrower, on average some 8 feet (2.5 m). First discovered a few decades ago, it is now certain that on the eastern section of the Wall the berm was covered in obstacles. Excavation has revealed a checkerboard pattern of three rows of pits, in which were set substantial posts, which in turn had sharpened stakes fixed into them (*cippi*). This presented a hedge

Limestone corner, where the Roman work party gave up after failing to break a number of granite boulders in the ditch of the Wall.

of spikes – an ancient equivalent of barbed wire. At several sites a low mound was found on the southern edge of the ditch, which would have made it difficult for anyone to crawl under the spikes or to cut at the base of the supports. Some sites show that the system was renewed during the third century. Like the ditch itself, these wooden obstacles were not expected to stop any attack, but they would slow the attackers down. Any attempt to hack through them was likely to be noisy, making them hard to get past stealthily, even at night.

The stone wall shows several variations in building style, including variants where foundations or lower courses of Broad Wall were completed in Narrow Wall. Foundations were usually of flagstones set in clay. The facing walls of squared rubble – or occasionally less finished stones – were usually bonded with limestone mortar and rarely with clay, while the core of stones, rubble and earth might be dry-stone, bonded with clay or more often bonded with mortar. In some cases an original dry-stone core was later replaced with mortar during one of the major repairs or rebuilds.

In the eighth century Bede wrote that the Wall 'is eight feet wide and twelve high, running in a straight line from east to west, as is plain for all to see even to this day'. Twelve feet (3.6 m) is higher than any sections surviving into the modern era, so this figure provides a bare minimum and estimates usually range between 12 and 15 feet (3.6–4.5 m). In milecastle 48 (Poltross Burn) there are stone steps which, when intact, would have reached to a similar height. It should be noted that this only tells us about the likely height of the wallwalk inside this milecastle. The Wall itself is unlikely to have been built to a uniform height along its entire length, especially in the central sector where it crosses the crags and successive narrow and deep re-entrants with very steep slopes. These may have required the Wall to run in a series of steps up or down, or perhaps to be higher to bridge the sudden dips in the landscape. It has also been suggested that it might have been higher in sections where the ditch was less deep than usual.[15]

With current evidence it is impossible to prove that the Wall itself had a walkway along its top like the ones in milecastles and forts. There is ample evidence for a string course of stones levelling the top of the Wall. This would be essential if the walkway existed, but in itself does not prove that there was one. One argument against a walkway is that the timber stockades constructed on other Roman frontiers did not have one and were simple barriers, and that this was also sometimes true of some of the dry-stone features built in sections of desert frontiers, such as in Africa. Against this we must set the width of the turf wall, which looks far more like a standard Roman army turf wall with walkway and parapet on top. In addition, even the Narrow Wall – and the few sections of extra Narrow Wall – would be excessively wide for a simple barrier not intended to carry a patrol walk, which would at every point allow one man to pass another. In the initial design the lack of a road close behind the Wall would have made a walkway the most convenient way for small parties to move along the line, while the foot-bridges across the rivers make most sense if they allowed this communication to continue. The nature of any parapet is conjectural, given that its very existence cannot be proven, but judging from evidence from Roman forts a battlement – perhaps with wider gaps than was common in medieval castles – is most likely.

If the Wall was some 15 feet (4.5 m) high, then most estimates of the height of turrets would place them at around double this, 30 feet (9 m). They did not project in front of the curtain. Trajan's Column and evidence from elsewhere suggests that many freestanding towers were built with tiled or shingle roofs and apparently a balcony running round all four sides. There is no direct evidence for either feature on Hadrian's Wall, and while

overleaf: The additional turret at Peel Gap shows the designers of the Wall's willingness to adapt the standard plan to local topography. As far as we know, there were always two turrets in between each milecastle in the original design of the Wall.

either or both are possible, the turrets may have been simple towers with open tops and parapets, giving good all-round visibility. Soldiers not on guard duty lived in the shelter of the room below, which was reached from ground level by a ladder, sometimes mounted on a low platform. As with milecastles, there was some flexibility in the positioning of turrets. There is also one known instance of an extra tower at Peel Gap, so that there are three between milecastles 39 and 40. This additional tower stands at the entrance of a pass which would have been out of sight of the other towers, and for men on a wallwalk unless they were at that moment at the pass itself. Discovered fairly recently, it raises the possibility that there were other exceptional features added to deal with local conditions.

Artefacts found in turrets suggest relatively short-term occupation with detachments probably spending only a few days and nights rather than weeks or months at these outposts, but there was time for soldiers to cook and gamble – this last shown by the presence of dice and gaming boards. Weapons, especially the iron heads from a range of spears and javelins, are fairly common. So far just one bolt head of the type shot by a light *ballista* – a twin armed catapult looking like a large crossbow – has been found in a turret. This raises the possibility that some or all turrets were equipped with one of these machines, often known as 'scorpions', which were highly accurate and propelled their missiles with great force. One theory based on the limited available data suggests that the berm in front of a turret was made deliberately narrower, so that the ditch almost abuts the Wall. This would have permitted men in the tower to see (and shoot) along the line of the ditch in each direction – something that would have been more difficult with the normal width of berm. However, this phenomenon is not seen on most of the surviving length of the ditch, and hopefully future excavation will reveal whether this was the standard layout or a local peculiarity.

Milecastles were considerably smaller than the independent outposts or fortlets usually built by the Roman army. Their side walls join the Wall itself at a right angle, but the southern corners are rounded on the outside like those of larger forts. Most are around 50 by 60 feet (15 x 18 m) in size, covering an area of some 3,000 square feet (270 sq m). A few are larger, with milecastle 47 and 48 nearer 60 by 70 feet (18 x 21 m) and covering an area of 4,200 square feet (378 sq m). The largest of all is the stone version that replaced the original turf milecastle 52 and covers some 6,932 square feet (644 sq m). Interestingly, its turf predecessor was also significantly larger than all other known milecastles on the turf wall and clearly the location was significant and felt to require a larger than normal presence. Little is known of the internal buildings in milecastle 52, but 47 and 48 were provided with a range of barracks on either side of the fort, as well as a stone oven built into the inside corner of the walls, and the famous steps in the case of milecastle 48, which have not been found at any other site. In spite of poor-quality stone used in the construction, these buildings are more substantial and appear to have been well furnished, even having glass in the windows. It seems likely that these larger milecastles pre-dated the decision to add forts to the Wall.

There is no trace of a standard plan to the internal structures in other milecastles, but these buildings usually appear cruder and suggest less accommodation for fewer soldiers. Garrisons of a dozen or so men may have been typical, with anything up to thirty or forty in the largest ones. A few finds of horse equipment hint at the presence of horses, and one or more cavalrymen in a garrison would make considerable sense, since this would permit messages to be sent more quickly to one of the forts. On the whole, the finds from milecastles suggest that soldiers spent more time there than at turrets, with a lot of evidence for food preparation and some for repair or manufacture of equipment. On other

HADRIAN'S WALL

frontiers, we hear of soldiers being sent to distant outposts for many months, but on the Wall a fort was never further than 4 miles (6.5 km) away, so that tours of duty in one of these little bases may well have been a lot shorter.

With one possible exception, every milecastle had a large entrance in the north and south walls. Solid construction suggests that a tower over the north gate was normal and it is possible that there was another over the south gate, although this appears less useful, since it would not have significantly increased all-round visibility. The towers in the north wall would have meant that, combined with the turrets, there was a raised viewing platform every third of a Roman mile (0.5 km). These gateways were substantial, the twin gates mounted on pivots, and provided a wide road through the Wall. In some cases the route was scarcely practical, for instance at milecastle 42 where it opens on to a 45-degree slope, which would have been difficult for men, very difficult for horses and impossible for ox- or mule-drawn vehicles. Milecastle 35 lies just south of a cliff dropping some 100 feet

opposite above: Reconstruction of milecastle 37.

opposite below: A cross section of the Wall and Vallum. From right to left (north to south) is the ditch, berm, Wall, the road or Military Way, north mound, Vallum ditch, south mound.

right: A cutaway view of a turret, in this case shown with a tiled roof. It is unknown whether these existed or whether the tops of towers were open to the elements.

(30 m) and thus would have been useless as a crossing place. This is the possible exception to the rule that all milecastles had two gates, for there is no clear trace of the northern one ever having been built. If so, then the planners of the Wall once again demonstrated a willingness to adapt the design to the topography.

All of the elements described so far were part of the original template for Hadrian's Wall before the decision was made to add forts and the subsequent addition of the Vallum. The latter was a huge obstacle to unauthorized crossing, most of all by cattle, sheep or horses, whether legitimately owned or stolen by raiders. The Vallum is difficult to understand, mainly because only a little excavation work has been done along it, but also because there is no close parallel to it from any other Roman frontier. Although essentially an earthwork, considerable care was taken in its construction. At the stretch running behind Limestone Corner the auxiliaries digging the ditch of the Vallum cleared it thoroughly, unlike the legionary work party who had left the ditch in front of the Wall unfinished.

Recent excavation has discovered no trace of the Vallum being recut or even routinely cleaned out, but it is hard to tell whether this was the case throughout its length. Opinion is also divided over whether the marginal mound was part of the original design, but more likely it was raised after the return from the Antonine Wall to block the causeways crossing the Vallum ditch. This was probably a simpler method than digging all the causeways out or refilling the gaps in the north and south mounds. Some have argued for an additional marginal mound on the north side of the ditch, but the evidence is confusing and uncertain.

The addition of forts to the line of Hadrian's Wall may well have rendered large milecastles unnecessary, and led to a reduction in size and garrison of those completed after this decision was made. The forts also rendered the crossings at all milecastles far less important, especially once the Vallum was dug

previous pages: This is one of many reconstructed Roman watchtowers from the frontier in Germany which might reflect the turrets on Hadrian's Wall.

and blocked access to and from the south. Where gaps were later cut to allow access from milecastles through the northern mound of the Vallum, there is no clear evidence for a route across the ditch and through the southern mound. Even so, it was decades before the north gates on many milecastles were reduced to simple doorways. The continued occupation of these outposts makes it clear that from then onwards they performed a useful function not connected with offering a path across the line of the Wall. If it is correct that milecastle 35 never had a north gateway, then this role had from the start been important. The demolition of many turrets suggests that these were no longer considered useful. This was especially common in the central section of the Wall, which lends further weight to the belief in a walkway. On such high ground, a sentry or patrol looking over the parapet from the Wall itself would have had only a slightly less good observation point than a man on top of a tower.

Forts and Towns: soldiers and civilians

The forts on the Wall offered the best routes across the Wall and Vallum, the latter as big an obstacle as the fortification itself. In addition, as already mentioned, there was definitely another major crossing at the Portgate, allowing Dere Street to continue to the north, and almost certainly one near Carlisle for the other major north–south road. Close to Housesteads, another gate was added at Knag Burn, which appears to date to the late second or early third century. This was surely under the control of the fort's garrison, and may have compensated for the inconvenient position of the fort's own northern gateway.

Towns flourished at Corbridge and Carlisle on the lines of the two main roads. These were substantial settlements by the standards of Roman Britain, if not quite on the same scale as the handful of big cities in the south of the province, let alone the grand cities of provinces like Gaul. In each case there was always a military presence and distinct military compounds, housing substantial detachments of legionaries, but this did not alter the essential civil character of the communities. The Vindolanda tablets make it clear that many traders and businessmen were drawn to the northern frontier c.100, and the long-term presence of so many soldiers created new markets, as did the people who came to profit from the military community. It is becoming clear that villas and large agricultural estates farming for profit were established further north in Roman Britain than we used to believe. Hadrian's Wall was very much part of the wider imperial economy, with goods and people coming in from all over the empire.

Traders followed the legions even on campaign, and almost as soon as an army base was established and occupied in the longer term civilian settlement swiftly started to cluster around it. As a fort became permanent, so did the community living around it, and it might eventually gain formal status as the *vicus* and some measure of self-government, the community acting together as the *vicani*. There were sometimes official buildings, such as the waystations or *mansiones* built to accommodate civil and military officials travelling on public business. A grand house outside the Hadrianic fort at Vindolanda was surely constructed for someone of importance, although the suggestion that it was built for the emperor himself during his inspection of the northern frontier is so far no more than an appealing conjecture. There is also evidence for army barracks in the *vicus* at Housesteads and Birdoswald at some periods, so that the area outside a fort was not always purely civilian.[16]

On the whole, most structures within the *vicus* were smaller and simpler than any official buildings. Access to the roads, especially the main road leading out of the fort, was at a premium, so that buildings tend to be narrow fronted and deep, a style we refer to as strip housing. The front often acted as a place of business, whether a shop or bar. There were also larger taverns and the like, as well as workshops and temples – much the same mix to be found in any normal town or large village, save for the lack of grand public buildings. Most *vici* were crowded and bustling, and many were large. Recent survey work at Housesteads has shown that the civilian settlement covered an area several times larger than the fort itself, with housing on both sides of the Vallum. Many may have been smaller than this, but even so were substantial. The early third century AD was the time when the *vici* of forts on Hadrian's Wall were at their height, and show every sign of prosperity with plentiful supplies of everyday goods coming from far afield. So far only two, at Wallsend and Housesteads, appear to have had a rampart and/ or ditch around them, with others simply being enclosed on one side by the Vallum and on the other by the Wall. At Maryport on the Cumbrian coast, the *vicus* was surrounded by a ditch.

Even when it covered a larger area outside the military compound, the *vicus* depended on the fort which provided the

reason for its existence. Wall forts conform in most respects to the typical design of Roman auxiliary forts in the western empire, shaped like a playing card with rounded corners and four gateways, one in each wall. The main gate, invariably double arched, led to the most important road in the fort, the *via praetoria*. This met the *via principalis* to form a T-junction, the second road running between the two side gates of the fort, and along it lay the key buildings of the base.

The *principia* (headquarters) stood at the junction of the roads. It was a very large courtyard complex, including an assembly hall, offices, storage space for the great quantity of records generated by the army, a strongroom (underground whenever possible) to keep its pay chest and other valuables, and the *aedes*, the shrine where the unit kept its standards alongside images of the emperor. The life of the unit was regulated and recorded in this building.

Next to the headquarters was the *praetorium* (the house of the garrison commander), which was often as large or even larger. Its design followed traditional Italian taste for the home of a rich man, and was based on the courtyard house surrounding a small central garden – ideal for offering cool shade in a hot Mediterranean summer. Living quarters, kitchens and other rooms were provided for the slaves and freedmen who performed much of the work needed to keep an equestrian gentleman in the style expected of someone of his rank. The Vindolanda tablets also make it clear that it was normal for the prefect to be accompanied by his family, so that women and children often lived at the heart of a fort. The tablets tell of birthday parties and other social occasions, where senior officers and their families visited each other. All in all they suggest a very comfortable lifestyle, and even in the timber phases these houses were large and well provided. When built in stone there was the prospect of even greater comfort, with a private bath suite and underfloor

Hadrian's Wall looking north-east from milecastle 36 towards Sewingshields Crags.

heating provided by hot air from a furnace blown through a hypocaust system.

More functional, but on an equally grand scale, were the *horrea* (granaries), which usually also lay on the *via principalis*. These are very distinctive structures, with huge buttressed walls and the floor raised by stone pillars or small walls. This was intended to deter vermin, but combined with the high ceiling also helped to regulate the temperature and so preserve the cereals and other foodstuffs stored inside. It was usual for the main entrance to be raised, making it easier to load and offload sacks, barrels and other bulky goods directly from a cart or wagon. Granaries most often occur as a pair, and it is striking that whenever a fort was wholly or substantially rebuilt on the same site the new granaries were not in the same place as the old ones. This suggests not only their importance, but also that the old buildings were kept in use for as long as possible until the new ones were ready.

A *valetudinarium* or hospital was provided in each fort, although as yet too little is known about the layout of these to make it easy to identify them; the courtyard building behind the *principia* at Housesteads may well be a hospital, but we cannot be sure. The strength report from Vindolanda lists thirty-one men in hospital, including six wounded, ten suffering from inflammation of the eyes, and fifteen others sick. Eye problems may well have been exacerbated from living in the dimly lit and smoky barrack blocks, and it is interesting that we hear of an effective eye-salve made from a range of ingredients including mercuric sulphide which was the work of an oculist in the British Fleet (*classis Britannica*) named Axius. One of the Vindolanda tablets mentions a *seplasiarius* or pharmacist, while others list medicines or their ingredients in lists of purchases. Army bases, much like ancient cities, were both crowded and periodically visited by individuals and groups from far afield, providing many opportunities for infections to spread, and one estimate suggests that the hospital in each base had the capacity to accommodate between 5 and 10 per cent of the whole garrison. Yet, on the whole, the army provided better medical facilities than were available to poorer civilians, and soldiers were as well cared for as the medical knowledge of the age permitted.

Much easier to identify from its remains than the military hospital is the *balneum* or bath-house. These were always of stone and always built outside the ramparts because of the risk of fire created by the furnaces, although since this meant that they were in the *vicus* there were sometimes other buildings nearby. Bathers went through a sequence of warm, very hot and cold rooms. Olive oil was used as soap and the skin then scraped clean with a *strigil*. There was also space for other activities, from exercise to board and dice games and simply talking and eating. That the bath-house was beyond the rampart may have added to the men's sense that they were off duty.[17]

The bulk of space within each fort was taken up with accommodation for troops, the number of buildings varying depending on the type of unit. An infantry barrack block was designed to house one century of eighty soldiers. It consisted of a long building, for much of its length divided into pairs of rooms, with each pair allocated to a *contubernium* of eight men, who on campaign would share a tent. Since there were ten *contubernia* in a century there ought to be ten pairs of rooms, but while this was sometimes true, other barrack blocks have slightly more or slightly fewer rooms. Assuming that we are correct to see a pair of rooms as accommodation for a *contubernium*, we have no idea of how the men slept, and bunk beds, straw palliasses or cots are all possible. Two or three men may have shared a cot or bed, an arrangement common for much of human history even if it seems deeply alien to those us born in the age of central heating. Hearths have been discovered on some sites, but do not appear to have been universal in all periods. At Vindolanda barrack room floors were covered in layers of rushes, heather and straw. When dirty, these were not cleared out and replaced, but simply covered with fresh material, leaving a thick mat of dirty and decaying vegetable matter. Finds of lost possessions, including objects as large as shoes, are common, which reinforces the sense of dimly lit and crowded barracks, rife with insects and other vermin, especially in the summer months. At one end the barrack block widened into a suite of rooms, which housed the centurion in greater comfort, probably with plastered and painted walls, and perhaps also had rooms for other junior officers such as the *signifer* (standard bearer).

As we have seen, around the 230s new barrack blocks were constructed which were smaller than the older pattern. These tend to have just five pairs of *contubernium* rooms, but are otherwise very similar in design. This appears to have occurred all along the Wall. One variation seen at some sites are the so-called 'chalet-barracks', where instead of a continuous range each *contubernium* occupies its own separate little building with side walls and roof and a narrow gap between the ones on either side. Presumably this was seen as easier to construct and maintain, for it does not seem to reflect any other change.

The stables required for the horses in the *cohortes equitatae* and *alae* remained something of a mystery until recently, when excavators at Wallsend identified several examples. Rather than a separate stable block, the Romans used a combined building similar in shape to a normal barrack block. Along one side was a row of rooms to accommodate the thirty or so troopers of a *turma*, each room usually equipped with a hearth. Backing on to these was a row of horse boxes, identified as such by the 'urine pits', shallow trenches below flooring which allowed liquid to drain into them. This was presumably to make it easier to clean out the stalls and replace the bedding. The rows of rooms on either side of the building do not connect, each one having to

One of the buttressed granaries at Housesteads gives an idea of the sheer scale of these functional buildings. Note the rows of pillars used to raise the floor above ground level.

be entered from the outside. This is reconstructed as a room on one side to house three troopers, with their three mounts in the adjacent (if unconnected) horse box. It is quite possible that there was an attic roof, providing further storage, and perhaps even living and sleeping space for the grooms, usually slaves, who assisted many cavalrymen in caring for mounts and equipment. As with infantry barracks, these buildings do not quite conform to what we would expect, having only nine sets of rooms instead of the ten that would have been required if there were thirty men and horses in a *turma*.

Like infantry barracks, the combined stable-barrack blocks had a suite of rooms at one end for its commander and other officers. However, these do not appear to include any stabling for the horses and it is unclear where officers' mounts were kept. Living so close together, a pervasive smell of horse sweat, manure, damp leather tack and saddles, straw and grain must have mixed with all the human scents of clothes, food and cooking. Any strongly garrisoned Roman fort was a very crowded place, with people and animals in close proximity, but most towns and cities were also very densely packed. It is also worth remembering that recruits to the auxiliary cavalry will often have come from rural communities in the provinces where people lived close to the land, with animals around them much of the time.

Slaves, including many owned by the army itself, known as *galearii* (helmet-wearers) and given a simple uniform and some training, added to the inhabitants of a fort, but were not the only non-combatants. From the time of Augustus Roman soldiers were not permitted to contract a legal marriage, until this ban was lifted by Septimius Severus some two centuries later. In the main this restriction allowed the state to accept no obligation to care for wives or children during or after a soldier's lifetime, for it is clear that in practice there was little effort to prevent men from forming long-term liaisons with women and raising families. Soldiers giving their origin as born 'in the camp' (*in castris*) were the products of such unions and readily accepted in the ranks once they were old enough to enlist. As far as the men were concerned, these were proper marriages. Hadrian passed a law making it easier for soldiers to bequeath property to their families, something that was clearly very important to them. On discharge, auxiliaries were granted citizenship not simply for themselves, but for one wife and the children the man had with her, an acknowledgement that many already were 'married'.

This raises the question of where soldiers' wives and children lived and the answer is not straightforward, perhaps because it varied from unit to unit and place to place. At Vindolanda there is clear evidence to show that the families were in the barracks with the soldiers, for objects associated with them, including shoes, are frequent finds in the rush and straw material used as flooring. Such things were clearly dropped and lost by the residents in these poorly lit buildings and were not dumped there as rubbish some time later. At other sites, such as Housesteads, there is no good evidence that women and children lived inside the fort itself. If a man's family lived in the *vicus* then it is hard to know how much time he would have been able to spend with them, or whether some or all were permitted to spend their nights outside the rampart of the fort. Centurions seem always to have been permitted to contract a marriage, and the rooms allocated to them in a barrack block may well have been a home to their families as well.

Looking at a plan of a Roman fort, it is the living space rather than the fortifications that stand out. When the *vicus* is included, the whole community looks far more like a garrison town than a purely military installation ready for war. This was where soldiers lived, worked, drilled, trained, ate, slept, relaxed, and raised families. The famous multi-seater latrine block at Housesteads, flushed by a flow of rainwater stored in tanks, gives one example

overleaf: A painting of Vindolanda *c.* AD 200, the fort lying on the same ground as the stone remains visible today.

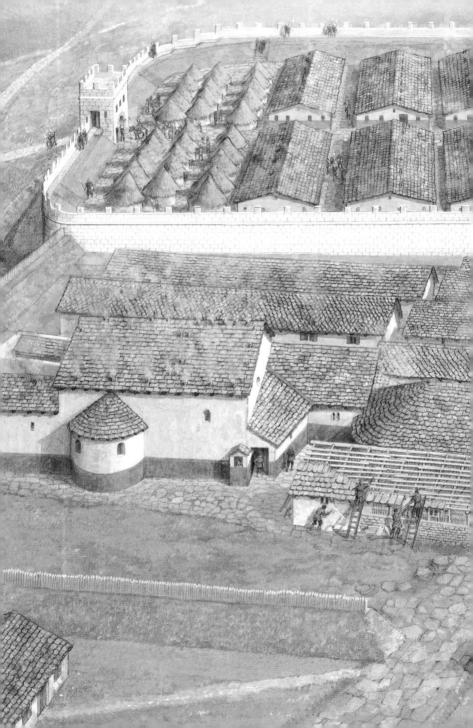

This full size reconstruction of a third century barrack block at South Shields gives a good idea of the appearance of soldiers' accommodation.

of a mundane activity carried out in a solidly constructed and purpose-built structure. There was a strongly urban feel to life in one of the army's bases. There were also a commonality of layout and design in the army's bases all over the empire and especially in the western provinces. Soldiers arriving at a garrison would see much that was familiar and reassuring.

Yet although forts were similar and recognizably of a kind, no two were identical and the fuller excavations carried out on some sites in recent years reveal successive redesigns which were often drastically different. At Vindolanda in the late second or early third century, there was a phase when an area either in the fort itself or a fortified annexe was occupied by people living in traditional Iron Age round houses. It is impossible to tell whether these were friendly local communities, hostages or prisoners, or a force of locals used as labour or soldiers who preferred to live in the traditional way. Around the time of Septimius Severus's campaigns in Scotland, South Shields was converted into a huge depot, with no fewer than twenty-two granaries within its walls. Positioned on the mouth of the Tyne, a port is presumed to have existed close to the fort, but has not yet been located. This huge supply base was part of the logistical support for the exceptionally large expeditionary force brought by Severus. Although overall troop numbers in the north declined after Severus, there were still substantial forces on and around the Wall, and South Shields probably continued to play an important role in supplying them for several generations.

Life on the Wall

It is highly likely that outbreaks of serious conflict in northern Britain go unmentioned in our meagre literary sources. Since there is good evidence for at least another major campaign under Hadrian apart from the one at the start of his reign, it is a safe bet that other unattested wars were also fought in the second century, let alone during the even more poorly recorded third and fourth centuries. Small-scale military operations are unlikely to appear in our sources even for well-documented periods. In the fourth century the soldier and historian Ammianus Marcellinus ended his account of some fairly minor operations in Gaul by saying that 'besides these battles, many others less worthy of mention were fought... which it would be superfluous to describe, both because their results led to nothing worthwhile, and because it is not fitting to spin out a history with insignificant details'.[18]

Warfare is underreported in our sources for the army on the Wall, but even so we can confidently state that it was an occasional or rare experience for most Roman soldiers. Even during a major campaign, many troops spent far more time marching and waiting, or drilling and preparing, than they spent in combat. Some men would never meet the enemy in battle or skirmish in their entire twenty-five years in the army, while others no doubt had more than their fair share of fighting. The bulk of a man's military service was spent in the routines of peace, with conflict a more or less distant prospect. Yet, for all that, Hadrian's Wall and the communities around it existed because of the army, and the regulations and habits of the Roman army were at the heart of life there.

In one sense the army never slept, for sentries were always on duty at any time of day or night, but its day formally started around sunrise with trumpet calls to rouse the garrison, and then parades and a gathering of officers in the *principia*. Among the Vindolanda tablets are many formulaic morning reports dating to the early years of the second century:

The administrative heart of a Roman fort was the *principia* or
headquarters building. This illustration shows the *principia* at
Housesteads in the second century AD.

Cutaway reconstruction of the second and larger bath-house built outside the fort at Vindolanda. Bottom left and without a connecting door to the main building is a latrine.

15th April. Report of *Cohors VIIII Batavorum*. All who should be are at duty stations, as is the baggage. The *optiones* and *curatores* made the report. Arcuttius, *optio* of the century of Crescens, delivered it.[19]

The *optio* was second-in-command to the centurion in charge of each century, while the *curator* fulfilled the same role for the decurion in charge of a *turma* of cavalrymen. It seems that one of them would act as spokesman for the day and deliver the report, which was based on a roll call taken of each sub-unit. Documents from other frontiers make it clear that a statement of overall numbers serving in the unit and their availability was given each morning and written down to be filed in the records. A new password for the day was issued, as well as other orders. A duty roster for a century from a legion stationed in Egypt records the fatigues assigned to its soldiers over a period of ten days, including such things as 'Gate guard', 'Baths', 'Escort to Centurion Serenus', 'Street cleaning' and 'Latrines'.

A soldier's entire career was tracked and recorded, from enlistment – 'Caius Longinus Priscus, aged 22, scar on left eyebrow' – to death or discharge: 'Released from service... Tryphon son of Dionysius... suffering from cataract and impaired vision.' The recording of animals acquired by the army was almost as full: 'enter in the records according to regular procedure a horse, four years old, reddish, masked, without brands, approved by me, assign it to Julius Bassus, trooper'.

Pay generated considerable documentation. Soldiers were supposed to be paid in three instalments each year, each of 100 silver *denarii* (or 400 of the smaller *sesterii*) for legionaries in Hadrian's day, although the rate received by auxiliaries is unclear. A pay return from Egypt gives a breakdown of the numerous deductions made from the money a soldier was supposed to receive. This dates to a time when legionaries received only

225 *denarii* a year, while auxiliary pay is unlikely to have been higher and may have been lower. Also, in this case the pay and accounting was done in the local drachma coin that was roughly the equivalent of the *sesterius*:

In the consulship of Lucius Asinius (AD 81)
QUINTUS JULIUS PROCULUS from DAMASCUS
Received the first salary instalment of the third year of the Emperor, 247.5 drachmas, out of which:

hay	10 drachmas
for food	80 drachmas
boots & straps (poss. socks)	12 drachmas
Saturnalia of the camp	20 drachmas
?	60 drachmas
expenditure=	182 drachmas
balance deposited to his account	65.5 drachmas
and had from before	136 drachmas
making a total of	201.5 drachmas

Received the second instalment of the same year 247.5 drachmas, out of which:

hay	10 drachmas
for food	80 drachmas
boots & straps (poss. socks)	12 drachmas
to the standards	4 drachmas
expenditure =	106 drachmas
balance deposited to his account	141.5 drachmas
and had from before	201.5 drachmas
making a total of	343 drachmas

Received the third instalment of the same year 247.5 drachmas, out of which:

hay	10 drachmas
for food	80 drachmas
boots & straps (poss. socks)	12 drachmas
for clothes	145.5 drachmas
expenditure =	247.5 drachmas
balance deposited to his account	343 drachmas

Other men show deductions made for lost or newly issued clothing and gear, but some of the charges, for instance for food, appear to be standard. Equally detailed accounts were kept for all the hundreds of men in every unit, giving some idea of the vast amount of documentation generated by the army and stored in the *principia* of each fort.

Apart from men and animals, equipment was also inspected, and a writing tablet from Carlisle dating to a generation before Hadrian's Wall deals with shortages in a cavalry *ala*, listing men *turma* by *turma*:

> Docilis to Augurinus his prefect greetings. As you ordered, we have attached below all the names of lancers who are missing lances, either who did not have fighting lances, or who [did not have] the smaller *subarmales* [probably a type of jerkin worn with a cuirass] or who [did not have] regulation swords.

Much documentation also followed the huge amounts of supplies required by the army. Another text from Carlisle lists the grain supplied to an *ala* of cavalry, in total 669 bushels of barley and 2,267 bushels of wheat, broken down into the amount allocated to each of the sixteen *turmae* in the unit.[20]

The number of soldiers actually present at a garrison varied considerably and is rarely likely to have matched its theoretical size and organization. A strength report of *Cohors I Tungrorum* stationed at Vindolanda in the late first century AD states that it had 752 men including 6 centurions on its books; a high proportion of its probable establishment of some 800 men. However, of these, only 296 and 1 centurion were at the fort, and 31 of these were unfit for duty. One centurion was in Londinium, two others off at other locations, each with a very small detachment of soldiers, while 45 men were on a long-term posting serving with the foot bodyguard of the provincial governor. The largest group of 337 men under 2 centurions was at Coria (almost certainly Corbridge), within a day's march, so relatively close. Flavius Ceralis, prefect of *VIIII Batavorum*, referred to Vindolanda as his 'winter-quarters' (*hiberna*), using a term familiar from Caesar, and it is likely that many units spent the colder months at their bases, but were often serving elsewhere in spring and summer.[21]

The same pattern of dispersal is reflected in other strength returns from units in other provinces, with officers and men away from their parent cohort or *ala*, sometimes a long way away, even in different provinces, and for significant periods of time. Wherever they were, the army's bureaucracy kept track of them. Milecastles and turrets needed manning by detachments and even if the distances involved were short and the men were not too far away from the main garrison, they were still not available instantly. The legionary presence at Corbridge and Carlisle, and perhaps at times other bases, brought men for months and perhaps longer up from the fortresses at Caerleon, Chester and York. Detachments or vexillations from legions in other parts of the empire came to northern Britain at times, and elements of the army of Britannia, presumably including units stationed on the Wall, were similarly posted away to other provinces as required.

Life in the garrison continued, however many or few soldiers were actually present. Records needed to be kept up to date, not least of pay and the issuing of equipment and rations, which in turn meant supervision of the granaries and stores. Most forts also had their workshops (*fabricae*), where weapons, armour, helmets, harness, horse fittings and saddles, tents and shield covers and a host of other things were manufactured and repaired, and soldiers were required to work in these and to run them. Horses could not spend all their time in their boxes, and needed to be exercised and cared for, as did the mules, ponies and oxen used as pack and draught animals. Some of these tasks were performed by the army slaves or personal slaves owned by some soldiers,

Cutaway reconstruction of the *praetorium* or commander's house at Housesteads in the second century AD. Apart from being built on a steep slope, this is typical of the houses occupied by the equestrian officers commanding auxiliary units.

especially cavalrymen, but much was done by the legionaries and auxiliaries themselves. Maintenance of the forts' buildings and the Wall and its other installations was a common task, with periodic new constructions or wholesale rebuilding creating bigger projects. Each task was underpinned by such things as tile making, quarrying and shaping stone, felling trees and working timber, as well as moving men and materials to where they were needed, so that behind the matter-of-fact inscriptions recording the erection or repair of a building lay a hive of activity.

Hadrian was an advocate of rigorous military training, as were all good emperors, and a series of inscriptions from North Africa record the speeches he gave to the units of the army there after watching them at manoeuvres. One cavalry *ala*:

> Filled the training ground with your wheelings, you threw spears not ungracefully, though with short and stiff shafts. Several of you hurled *lancea* spears with skill. Your jumping onto horses was lively and yesterday swift. Had anything been lacking, I would note it... You pleased equally throughout the whole manoeuvre.

Afterwards he watched the horsemen from a *cohors equitata*, who were paid less and were less well mounted than the prestigious cavalry in the *alae*. Hadrian began by telling them that:

> It is hard for the horsemen of a cohort to please, even as they are, and harder still not to displease after a show by the horsemen of an *ala*: the training field differs in size, spear throwers are fewer... the build of horses and the shine of weapons in keeping with the pay level. But you have banished weariness by your eagerness, by doing briskly what had to be done. Moreover, you both shot stones from slings and fought with javelins; everywhere you jumped nimbly onto your horses.

Praise was occasionally leavened with constructive criticism, for instance when some archers were too slow in forming into ranks, and some cavalry pursued too fast during a mock battle so that they fell into disorder.[22]

No doubt long preparation underlay the good performance of the army in Africa, since they were likely to have had plenty of warning of an imperial visit and to have done their best to impress him. Provincial legates were expected to inspect the troops under their command and report on their condition, but time and opportunity for all types of training had to compete with many other demands on soldiers' time as well as the tendency for units to be heavily under strength and dispersed over a wide area. In ideal conditions there was an emphasis on physical fitness and individual weapon-skills – fencing at a post and sparring with an opponent; throwing javelins; shooting at targets for archers; while cavalry practised vaulting into and out of the saddle (something especially important before the invention of the stirrup), horsemanship, and throwing javelins on the move. A cow skull from Vindolanda was put on a post and used as a target by soldiers practising with a *scorpio* or small, bolt-shooting *ballista*.

However, in general it is hard to identify the army's parade grounds and training areas archaeologically, so we do not know much about where such activities took place. Literary sources also speak of group training, including route marches, formation drill, building temporary camps and mock battles. Josephus, who as one of the leaders of the Jewish Revolt in the first century AD fought against the Romans, spoke of an army always preparing for war and claimed that their 'drills were bloodless battles and their battles bloody drills'. One of the provincial governor's duties was to inspect the units under his command and report on their state, ordering any problems to be rectified. The ideal state of readiness was seldom achieved, for it was a question of balancing all the tasks given to the army with keeping it ready for its military role. More than once the Romans were caught unprepared if a major war developed unexpectedly. If they had advance warning, then this was the time for intensive training to bring units to a much higher state of readiness.[23]

Whether training, writing and filing documents, building a road, repairing a spearhead or cleaning out the latrines, soldiers needed to eat and rest. The army issued a daily ration of grain, usually wheat, often supplemented by meat, such as beef, mutton or bacon. Legionaries seem to have received more pork than auxiliaries, reflecting traditional Italian tastes even though by Hadrian's reign very few soldiers were recruited into the legions from Italy. Bone finds from auxiliary forts, including those on the Wall, show auxiliaries eating substantial amounts of beef, but even more mutton and lamb, much of this probably found locally. Most troops had a mixed diet of meat and vegetables, especially lentils, although analysis of the drain from a latrine at Bearsden on the Antonine Wall suggested that its garrison was almost wholly vegetarian.

Food was issued raw or unprepared, so that for instance it was up to the soldiers to grind the grain to flour and cook it. Often this was done as a group by the men who shared a pair of barrack rooms, perhaps assisted by slaves if they owned them or their wives if they had them. There was no equivalent to the canteen or mess hall, and men ate in and around the barracks. The army had two basic meals in the day, breakfast (*prandium*) in the morning and dinner (*classicum*) at the end of the day. Wine was issued, usually the sour vinegar-like *acetum* or the cheap *posca*, although beer (*cervesa*) appears to have been more popular, especially with troops recruited from northern Europe. One of the Vindolanda tablets consists of a letter written by a decurion to his prefect asking for orders, but at the end adds: 'My fellow soldiers have no beer. Please order some to be sent.' On campaign hard-tack biscuit or *bucellatum* and salted bacon were common.[24]

Diet was supplemented by hunting and fishing, where this was possible, and by the purchase of extras, including better wine, fruit, eggs, meat of various sorts, fish and oysters. A great variety of products was available to be bought in the forts and *vici* and in towns like Corbridge and Carlisle. Requests for leave are common among the Vindolanda tablets, and it is unclear whether these were for long periods and meant to allow an auxiliary to return to his homeland in the Netherlands, or short passes to visit a much closer town and enjoy its pleasures. After the Wall had been built, the population of the whole area grew considerably, making even more goods and services available to soldiers who were careful to save their pay. Officers and their households inevitably ate better and more exotic food than the ordinary soldiers. One of the Vindolanda tablets was written by the slave Severus, to another slave, Candidus, owned by the prefect Genialis, arranging for him to purchase goods which included radishes. Another letter, again probably from slave to slave, gave instructions for the purchase of a range of goods needed by a large household, including:

> Bruised beans, two *modii*, chickens, twenty, a hundred apples,
> if you can find nice ones, one hundred or two hundred eggs,
> if they are for sale at a fair price... 8 *sextarii* of fish sauce...
> a *modius* of olives.[25]

While those of lower ranks were less able to afford so many luxuries, it is striking just how many types of food, drink and other goods were widely available on Hadrian's Wall and other outposts of the empire. Soldiers generally owned more than one pair of shoes, with boots for their uniform, lighter shoes for indoors and wooden sandals for going to the bath-house with its heated floors. This is in contrast to the Middle Ages, when most people owned just a single pair of shoes, only replacing them when they were worn out. Even in the late first and early second century, the Vindolanda tablets show an army base fully connected to the long-distance trade that flourished under the empire.

Wallsend

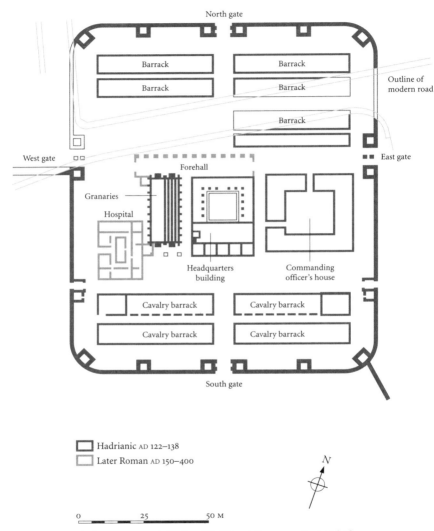

North gate

Barrack

Barrack

Barrack

Barrack

Outline of
modern road

Barrack

West gate

Forehall

East gate

Granaries

Hospital

Headquarters
building

Commanding
officer's house

Cavalry barrack

Cavalry barrack

Cavalry barrack

Cavalry barrack

South gate

Hadrianic AD 122–138

Later Roman AD 150–400

N

0   25   50 M

As its name suggest, Wallsend fort lies at the very eastern end of
Hadrian's Wall, where the Wall stops on the bank of the River Tyne,
not far from its mouth. It was constructed to house a *cohors equitata*
with a theoretical strength of 480 infantry and 120 cavalry.

The *vici* outside forts offered inns where men could eat and drink, play board or dice games and gamble, and no doubt engage the services of prostitutes. In the civilian community around Housesteads excavation has revealed loaded dice, traces of the forging of coins and murder, all within yards of the rampart of the fort. The murder victims were an ageing couple buried beneath the floor of one of the houses. Presumably at the time they simply vanished, since their remains were only uncovered by archaeologists, and the same is true of the boy whose skeleton was discovered under the floor of a barrack block at Vindolanda.[26]

No doubt life on Hadrian's Wall could be brutal and was often bawdy and rough, but we should not push this image too far, for this was a zone regulated by the army. A merchant who had been beaten by soldiers felt able to complain to a senior officer at Vindolanda, most likely the prefect, and clearly believed that this was worthwhile and might bring some form of recompense. Plenty of civilians were drawn to the area and made prosperous lives for themselves, while discharged soldiers chose to stay close to where they had served. A man named Barates came from Palmyra (in modern Syria), an oasis city on the Silk Road, and was either a serving or former soldier or perhaps a merchant supplying standards to the army. At some point he bought a slave woman named Regina – Queen or Queenie – who was a Briton from the Catuvellauni who lived north of the Thames. He freed her and married her, and when she died he set up an expensive monument depicting her sitting in a wicker chair and dressed as a proper Roman matron. The text is mainly in Latin, but at the bottom he had added in the curving script of his own Semitic dialect, 'Regina, the freedwoman of Barates, alas.'[27]

Tombstones testify to an ethnically diverse community, but also to familiar and natural human emotions, as people commemorated friends, husbands, wives, lovers or comrades. Monuments to children are among the most poignant, such as the one to a five-year-old girl with the somewhat Germanic name 'Ahtela', a six-year-old 'very dear daughter' Julia Materna, or 'Ertola, properly called Vellibia, who lived most happily four years and sixty days', whose tombstone bears a childlike picture of her holding a ball. At South Shields a father set up this memorial to his son, 'Sacred to the spirits of the departed: Au...dus lived nine years, nine months; Lucius Arruntius Salvianus [set this up] to his deserving and most devoted son.' The same site produced another monument to 'Victor, a Moorish tribesman, aged 20, freedman of Numerianus, cavalryman in *ala I Asturum*, who most devotedly conducted him to his tomb.' The dead young man is depicted reclining at a feast, and it is impossible to know whether he was a fondly regarded servant or a lover.[28]

Religion and ritual were everywhere in the ancient world, and many inscriptions are religious in nature, with altars dedicated to gods and goddesses from all over the empire. Especially common are the guardian deities of Rome itself, revered as part of the official annual rituals of the army and state. Substantial, well-carved altars dedicated to Jupiter Optimus Maximus ('best and greatest') often bear the names of a senior officer and his unit and may well have been dedicated at a formal parade. For instance, 'To Jupiter, Best and Greatest, Lucius Cammius Maximus, prefect of cohors *I Hispanorum equitata*, willingly and deservedly fulfilled his vow.'[29]

Others are far more personal, although no less expensive. The *mithraeum* or Temple to Mithras at Carrawburgh gives an idea of the dark, cavern-like shrines where this eastern god was worshipped. Mithraism was a mystery religion, its devotees sworn to secrecy about its rites and initiated to ever more senior levels in a cult which stressed manly virtues. It appears to have had particular appeal to equestrian officers, and perhaps was a useful way to make connections with other men of a similar rank, as well as an emotionally satisfying experience. The main altars

The tombstone of Ertola, properly named Vellibia, who lived happily for four years and sixty days. It has a child-like image of the little girl holding a ball, four fingers and a thumb shown on each hand because every child knows that that is how many should be there.

125

from this temple have a similar formal tone to other dedications by equestrian commanders of auxiliary units. 'To the invincible god Mithras Lucius Antonius Proculus, prefect of *cohors I Batavorum Antoninianae* willingly and deservedly fulfilled his vow.'[30]

Nearby is the shrine to the goddess Coventina (or sometimes Covventina) and the nymphs, a temple built around a natural spring. It has yielded a good number of inscriptions, but remains hard to pin down, and opinion is divided over whether she was already a local deity when the Romans arrived or was imported from one of the Celtic parts of the empire. Combining local gods and goddesses with Greco-Roman equivalents was fairly common, so that we have Vinotonus, the god of the hunt, renamed as Silvanus, and the related Cocidius who was equated with Mars. The outpost fort at Bewcastle was called *Fanum Cocidii* and appears to have enclosed an existing place of worship for the local population, probably to allow the Romans to regulate tribal gatherings. In spite of the suppression of the Druidic cult by the Romans in the first century AD, there is little sign of a direct clash between belief systems in northern Britain. In most cases local religions were not seen as incompatible with the culture and religion of the empire, since for polytheists the addition of new gods and goddesses presented few problems. The druids were a rare exception to this, partly because the Romans were disgusted by their practice of human sacrifice, and also because as a priesthood with authority beyond that of tribes and local leaders, they had the potential to unite Britons in opposition to Rome. As a consequence the religion was outlawed, and its most sacred shrines destroyed when the Roman army raided the island of Mona (modern Anglesey) in AD 60. Such direct conflict with a religious group was rare, but that is not to say that Roman appropriation of native cults and shrines represented a mutual and willing coming together of cultures. The locals may well have ignored many of the Roman versions of their cults, but were permitted to continue their traditional practices.[31]

There is little direct evidence for Christianity on Hadrian's Wall until well into the fourth century, but this is generally true of Roman Britain and thus unsurprising. The early Church is hard to detect archaeologically, for it set up very few inscriptions and it was not until much later that buildings recognizable as churches began to be built. It seems reasonable to assume that there were Christians as individuals and organized churches on the Wall as there were in most of the empire, at first on a small scale, but gradually becoming more common. Once the Emperor Constantine adopted the new religion, Christians became considerably more visible as part of the wider community. There is evidence for a very large building which was quite probably a church outside the fort at Maryport on the Cumbrian coast in the later fourth century, and there may have been smaller churches at Vindolanda, Housesteads and South Shields.

Altars and temples can survive as tangible traces of beliefs and rituals, but many other aspects of daily life leave little or no archaeological trace. One of the most striking features of the Vindolanda tablets is the normality of garrison life and trade on Britain's northern frontier, and especially the social life of unit commanders and their families:

> Claudia Severa to her Lepidina greetings. On 11 September, sister, for the day of the celebration of my birthday, I give you a warm invitation to make sure that you come to us, to make the day more enjoyable for me by your arrival, if you are present [?]. Give my greetings to your Cerialis. My Aelius and my little son send him [?] their greetings. I shall expect you, sister. Farewell, sister, my dearest soul, as I hope to prosper, and hail.

If life was settled enough for such pleasantries a generation before Hadrian's Wall, then it was surely at least as secure for much

Close to Carrawburgh fort is the natural spring and temple to
Covventina (or sometimes Coventina) and the nymphs. A large
number of dedications and votive offerings have been found at the site,
which drew worshippers from soldiers and the wider civilian
community on the Wall.

of the time after its construction, when far more troops were concentrated in the area. Equestrian officers and their wives were the most senior people living for years on end in the forts on the Wall or the outposts beyond it. The wife of one prefect at High Rochester north of the Wall was a senator's daughter. She would have run their extensive household just as she would have done at home, managing slaves and freedmen as well as overseeing the education and care of her own children. If comforts were a little less than in settled provinces, and certainly great public entertainments and festivals were rare events and smaller in scale, these women, like their husbands, were still living a generally familiar version of the lifestyle of their class. The same was true of the junior officers and their families, and of the soldiers and civilians in and around the forts. Life on Hadrian's Wall was in most respects much like life in the rest of the Roman empire, and people wore similar clothes, adopted the same fashions, and no doubt told the same stories and sang the same songs, as people elsewhere.

How Hadrian's Wall Worked: understanding the evidence

Hadrian's Wall forced peaceful travellers to cross at either a milecastle – in the initial design – or later at a fort or one of the small number of other gates. This permitted the Roman authorities to monitor everyone who came through the military zone, allowed them to refuse passage if they chose, and levy a toll on those who did cross if this was felt appropriate. All of this mirrors the army's supervision of movement in other frontier regions or sensitive areas, for instance the routes to and from the ports on Egypt's Red Sea coast. In the case of northern Britain, we cannot say how many civilians routinely crossed the Wall, who they were, or what business they had. When the Wall was abandoned and the Antonine Wall established instead, it is striking how much effort went into slighting the Vallum and making crossing-places over it, and also into removing gates at milecastles. This does suggest that there was enough traffic through the line of the Wall to make all this worthwhile, but it does not tell us any more about who these travellers were or why they wanted to cross. Nevertheless, it is hard to imagine that the Romans would have gone to such lengths to build the Wall and to maintain and man it for the best part of 300 years if its sole purpose was as a grand customs barrier.

The presence of so many soldiers makes it clear that there was a perceived and serious military threat, which meant that Hadrian's Wall was recommissioned after the decision to abandon the Antonine Wall. There would have been no need to do this had the Wall been simply the vanity project or grand architectural statement of Hadrian. Yet the Roman army was designed for mobile warfare and not static defence. Its doctrine was aggressive, both at the strategic and tactical levels, relying on its superior command and control, discipline, training and equipment to give it an advantage over all opponents, and especially a tribal army consisting of a small number of semi-professional warriors backed by a mass of enthusiastic but untrained and undisciplined tribesmen. The larger a tribal army became, the harder it was for its leaders to control and manoeuvre, magnifying all of the Romans' advantages, so that often small Roman columns were able to defeat numerically far larger enemy armies.

In all its phases, Hadrian's Wall was designed to allow the Roman army ready access across its line. By the third century, more than a quarter of the soldiers stationed in or near the Wall were cavalrymen, with three ordinary *alae*, and a larger, elite milliary *ala*, the *ala Petriana* at Stanwix, as well as the horsemen in the mixed cohorts and some irregulars. Such a strong force of high-quality cavalrymen allowed the army to patrol far in advance of the Wall, and even well beyond its outpost forts. They acted as a reminder of Roman strength and of the army's long reach, while providing intelligence of the mood of the local tribes and leaders. More information came from allies, spies and informers. Diplomatic activity was equally vital, whether ensuring goodwill through payment of subsidies to native leaders, and meetings allowing Roman representatives to gauge chieftains' moods and ask about their neighbours. On other frontiers we hear of centurions sitting in at tribal councils, while the Vindolanda tablets mention men with the title of *centurio regionarius*, who probably were responsible for dealings with the locals in a set area.

Major wars were rare, and through all these sources of information the army hoped to have plenty of warning when they were brewing. If more urgent diplomacy, threats and bribes then failed to deal with the situation, the army mustered one or more columns from the troops available, and marched out to confront and defeat any enemies in the open. Far more often than not, this was successful. Problems arose only if the enemy proved stronger and more skilful than expected, or – and this was a bigger risk – the garrisons of the Wall zone were depleted, overstretched, undertrained or badly led. Then there was a risk of defeat and ignominious retreat.

Hadrian's Wall was not designed to withstand attack by a large and determined hostile army, for it was too long for the defenders to be strong at every point. Given that it was most likely to be attacked when its garrisons were weaker than usual and incapable of defeating the enemy well in advance of the Wall, this problem of a defending force stretched out too thinly to defend such an extensive position only became worse. A strong attacking force would be able to overwhelm the defences at a given point and seize one of the gateways. The blocking up of many milecastle gateways forced attackers towards the forts or major crossings, which were better protected, but since any trouble was likely to occur at a time of weakness this was not in itself always enough to prevent their capture. Hadrian's Wall would not stop a strong enemy force, but it would slow it down. It took time and perhaps casualties to seize a crossing, and then more time to pass through gateways and cross the Vallum.

These delays provided the Romans with more time to recover and to bring troops from elsewhere in the province – or from the rest of the empire – so that eventually they had a strong enough force to defeat the enemy in open battle. How long this took depended on the wider situation, and at times of military crisis on other frontiers, and even more during the frequent civil wars of the third and fourth centuries, it might be many months or years before an effective military response was possible.

Most of the time, the Romans were sufficiently strong that the Wall and its garrison, combined with an active diplomatic presence further north, either deterred major attacks or dealt with them effectively in the field. Smaller-scale aggression was a different matter, and when we consider this the design of the Wall makes a good deal more sense. Raiding was common in most Iron Age societies and was the most frequent type of warfare. The communities north of Hadrian's Wall were loosely organized, and a treaty with a tribe did not automatically bind all chieftains or

Painting of a Roman auxiliary cavalryman based on a tombstone found
at Lancaster in Northern England in 2005.

individuals within the group to keep the peace. A successful raid brought profit from plunder, whether goods, livestock or captives as slaves, and also glory, demonstrating the might of a leader and his followers.

Hadrian's Wall was a barrier to unauthorized crossing, while its garrison provided substantial numbers of soldiers, many of them mounted, to hunt down and engage any raiding band. In normal circumstances it would be just a matter of time before attackers were intercepted. The Wall helped to give the Romans the time to respond. Even before an attack it made it much harder for spies to cross and find suitable targets for the raid. On other frontiers, many tribes were only allowed to attend a few markets held on or the near the frontiers, and it was a privilege and mark of trust to be permitted to travel more widely within the empire. Without prior information of where to find farms, villas, temples or other sources of spoils, raiders had to spend time during the attack to find what they wanted.

Getting across Hadrian's Wall was not easy, as the ditch, obstacles and the lie of the land slowed attackers down. The Wall itself might be climbed by men, but it blocked the path for horses, restricting mobility on the other side. From the start there was the risk of being spotted by patrols north of the Wall, and even more while trying to get across it. Large bands were inevitably more visible. A handful of men might sneak across, but if they were seen then even the small detachment at a turret, or a few men patrolling the Wall itself (assuming there was indeed a walkway) could delay and inflict casualties on them. After the Wall there was the Vallum to cross, bringing more delay and even greater chance of being observed. Bigger bands might fight their way across, overwhelming the men at a milecastle and crossing there, but this was hard to do without raising the alarm.

The Wall could be crossed in secret, especially under cover of darkness, or in low visibility during fog, heavy rain or snow, although even in these circumstances there was a risk of being seen. A simple alert – whether from a beacon, flag signal or despatch rider – warned the nearest garrisons of danger, allowing them to prepare a response and to start sending out scouts to find out more information. A plundering raid left a trail in its wake, of attacked settlements, ambushed travellers, and stolen flocks or herds. The more destructive a raid was, then the more visible it became: smoke from a burning farm was as good as a beacon for raising the alarm.

Even success brought its own problems. Plunder had to be transported, slowing the raiders down to the pace of burdened men if they carried what they had taken, or to the speed of pack or draught animals if they loaded it on to these. Stolen animals had to be herded, human captives watched to prevent escape, while valuable prisoners such as women and children might not be able to move at the fast pace set by warriors. Booty of all kinds was only of value if it could be carried home to safety, but successful raiders inevitably moved more slowly on the way back than on the way in. If they had acquired pack animals or carts then these had to be got across any rivers in their path, let alone the Vallum and Wall itself. All the while, the Romans were hunting them. Time and again on all frontiers the Roman army was unable to prevent all raiders from getting into the provinces, but often caught them and destroyed them as they turned for home. An altar probably from Corbridge recorded just such an interception: 'Quintus Calpurnius Concessinius, prefect of cavalry, after slaughtering a band of Corionototae, fulfilled his vow to the god of most efficacious power.'[32]

This is the only mention of the Corionototae, so we do not know where they came from or how numerous and aggressive a people they were, assuming that the prefect had identified them correctly.

Housesteads

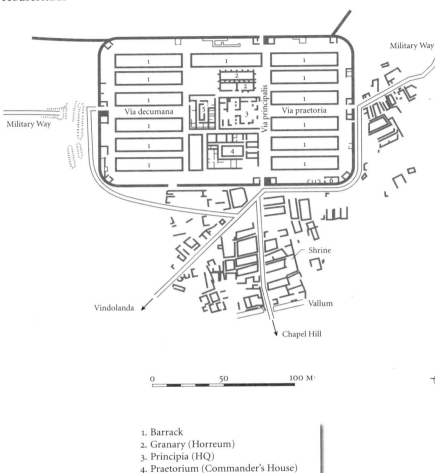

1. Barrack
2. Granary (Horreum)
3. Principia (HQ)
4. Praetorium (Commander's House)
5. Hospital?
6. Latrine

Housesteads provides direct evidence that the decision to add forts to the Wall was made not only after the initial design, but after substantial work had already been completed, because it required the demolition of a turret on the Wall.

As long as Hadrian's Wall was reasonably well garrisoned, it made successful raids across it very difficult. Some attackers may have circumvented the Wall and come by sea, hence the installations along the Cumbrian coast designed in similar manner to spot any bands and allow them to be caught. Every raid intercepted and either captured or destroyed helped to frighten other potential attackers, just as every band that escaped with plunder encouraged others to try their luck. Another deterrent was the threat of Roman reprisals, effectively raids of their own, reaching north from the military zone and striking with dreadful force against the communities held responsible for attacks. The closest settlements were especially vulnerable, but the Romans were fully capable of assembling a large column and marching far to the north, even beyond the Forth–Clyde line.

Raiding was a problem encountered by the Romans on many frontiers. Hadrian's Wall took advantage of the comparatively narrow neck of land between the Tyne and Solway to make entering and leaving the settled part of the province very hard, but in other respects its approach was conventional. Ultimately its success rested less on the fortifications and barriers than on the soldiers who manned them. Everything, from spotting raids to repelling them, to sending punitive expeditions north as a reprisal, and the ability to confront and defeat any large tribal army, relied on a numerous, well-trained and prepared military presence. At times this was lacking, and led to disasters, for instance in 367 when some of the scouts and spies employed by the army were found to be in league with raiders, but for the greater part of three centuries this military dominance was maintained in northern Britain by the Roman empire.

Changing Times and the End of Empire

In addition to the cohorts and *alae*, various irregular units appear on Hadrian's Wall during the course of the third century AD, such as the band or *numerus* of Hnaudifridius at Housesteads, or 'the German citizens of Twenthe' serving in the column or *cuneus* of Frisians at the same fort. Pottery shows extensive presence of Germanic tribesmen and their families cooking in traditional ways at this base, with some hint that they may have lived in a distinct part of the *vicus* rather than inside the fort. The Romans had a long tradition of recruiting warriors from recent enemies and posting them to a distant frontier, thus removing a potential source of trouble. Irregular units like this appear to have been commanded by their own leaders, such as Hnaudifridius, rather than equestrian officers, and were most likely cheaper to raise. It is hard to say how much training their soldiers received, and whether they looked and fought more like warriors than soldiers. Such units may have helped boost troop numbers on the Wall after the reduction in the size of cohorts and *alae* in the 230s, but by their nature they were less permanent. Similar allied and irregular units became more common throughout the empire around the same time.

This was only one of the wider changes which altered the nature of the army on the Wall. In 212 Caracalla extended Roman citizenship to the overwhelming majority of free inhabitants of the empire, which meant that many auxiliaries were now citizens. This status was less of an advantage than it had been in the past, since the law increasingly distinguished between citizens who were *honestiores* or 'the more honest or honourable men', who were generally the rich and received far more lenient treatment, and the majority of *humiliores* or 'more humble men', subject to harsher punishment for the same offences and with fewer rights. At times soldiers were pampered by emperors eager to buy and keep their loyalty, given donatives or special payments to celebrate accessions and imperial successes or landmarks. This did not prevent many from defecting to support popular or more generous commanders in the long cycle of civil war and usurpation. Decades of inflation reduced the value of regular military pay, so that it is a mistake to see all soldiers as privileged members of society. By the late third century more and more soldiers were conscripts rather than volunteers. Later, military service was made compulsory for the sons of soldiers, and the punishments for draft dodgers became ever more severe. When some resorted to cutting off a thumb so that they could not hold a sword or shield, it was decreed that the state would accept two thumbless men in place of one with intact hands.

As the third century progressed, the remaining distinctions between legionaries and auxiliaries as well as the differences in equipment gradually faded. Over the course of the third century the distinctive banded armour (known to scholars as *lorica segmentata*) worn by many legionaries fell into disuse, as did the *pilum*. By the later third century legionaries and auxiliaries alike wore mail or scale armour, carried oval shields, and fought with a range of spears and javelins. Around the same time the long *spatha* sword, in the past used by the cavalry, was adopted by infantry as well, replacing the famous *gladius* short sword. Some troops also employed lead weighted darts or *plumbatae*, several of which were sometimes carried clipped on to the back of the shield. By the fourth century legions were much smaller units than in the past, probably numbering little more than 1,000 to 1,200 men, making them only slightly bigger than the milliary cohorts of the *auxilia*. A lot of military equipment was now produced by state-owned factories rather than at army bases themselves, and assumes a simpler, mass-produced and more uniform appearance. Clothing styles changed as well, with long-sleeved tunics and long trousers becoming universal, so that even emperors dressed in this way on campaign.

As the army and empire changed, local developments continued. Around the beginning of the fourth century, the outpost forts were abandoned and there were major changes in the nature of the forts on Hadrian's Wall itself. The *vici* had flourished for some time, only to shrink and then vanish almost completely, perhaps as early as *c.*280 and certainly by the start of the fourth century. At Vindolanda, a temple to Jupiter Dolichenus was built inside the fort in the third century, something that would have been unimaginable in earlier periods. During the fourth century there is also clear evidence for civilian presence inside the fort, including an area apparently used as a market, something which appears to be mirrored at other sites. It looks very much as if garrisons had become smaller. This in itself is likely over time to have reduced the numbers of people living in the *vici*, contributing to the disappearance of these settlements, as the civilians who continued to form part of the military community moved inside the fort. At the same time many goods from the wider Roman world cease to be found in the forts, suggesting the decline and eventual cessation of much long-distance trade. Coins are common, but were by this time usually of low value, and the impression is of smaller numbers of soldiers who were less able to afford luxuries. There is no more new samian pottery or amphorae containing olive oil, products that were common in the past, even though they had been brought from outside the province. In contrast, towns like Corbridge and Carlisle continued to thrive, so some merchants may well have moved to these larger communities.

South Shields was rebuilt early in the fourth century, with its buildings situated around a central crossroad. In this sense it was a break from the traditional fort layout, but the ten barracks were very similar to their small third-century predecessors, as was the *principia*. The *praetorium* was in the south-east quarter of the fort, but was the familiar Mediterranean-style courtyard house, and was occupied until *c*.370 or 380. Wherever the men who commanded the fort came from, they clearly expected to live in the style of an Italian gentleman just as their predecessors had done.

Yet elsewhere there are signs that the army lacked some of the skill and resources of earlier periods. When the north wall of the fort at Housesteads became unsound, it was repaired by piling an earth bank against it and over it. Similar earth and timber repairs were carried out at Vindolanda and Birdoswald. In the last few decades of the fourth century, the arrangement of barracks in several forts became less ordered, with living accommodation taking the form of small structures no longer so neatly arranged in rows, and instead haphazardly laid out. When the courtyard *praetorium* at South Shields fell out of use, it was not replaced by a similarly grand structure. At Birdoswald, one granary collapsed and was not rebuilt, while its companion was modified, the raised floor being taken up and the ground beneath filled before a new floor was laid, presumably because it was no longer used to store grain in a controlled temperature. Other sites also show the abandonment or conversion of granaries for other purposes, and where new granaries were built they tended to be smaller. This suggests that it was no longer normal to store such large quantities of food in a fort, and is likely to reflect smaller garrisons, even when civilians are included, and a reliance on local supply.

Some of the changes visible on Hadrian's Wall echo wider developments in the Roman empire. Septimius Severus had divided Britain into two provinces, most likely through fear that an ambitious governor might copy his example and fight his way to power. From then on, no province contained more than two legions. This desire to prevent any one official from holding too much authority was taken much further in the later third and fourth centuries. Septimius Severus treated senators with great

overleaf: The Roman granaries at Birdoswald were rebuilt in the fifth century as timber chieftain's halls.

suspicion and gave a number of senior posts to equestrians instead; this trend increased during the third century, until eventually senators ceased to hold military posts at all. Equestrians commanded legions and provinces, and in time most emperors were former equestrian officers. By the fourth century Britain had become four (and perhaps later five) provinces, and in each one military command was separated from civilian administration. In addition, the army was divided into two, the *comitatenses* or 'mobile field units' and the *limetanei* or 'frontier garrisons', which included the men on Hadrian's Wall. Each of these had wholly separate command structures. The result was to make it difficult for anyone to marshal the resources of a province to deal with any major problem. Only when an emperor took an interest was anything likely to be done.

Rarely was this the case, for Roman rivals always took priority over the security of the empire. More than once in the third century, Britain split away under the rule of emperors whose power did not encompass the entire empire. Carausius was one of the most successful of these rulers, but – like so many emperors in this period – he was eventually murdered and replaced by one of his own officers, a man named Allectus. In 296 Constantius I invaded Britain, killing Allectus and making a triumphal entry into London. Constantius was Caesar in the western provinces and one of the tetrarchs, a group of four men sharing imperial rule. From now on it was usual for there to be more than one emperor at a time, even on those rare occasions when there was no challenger claiming power somewhere in the empire. Constantius stayed in Britain for a while, and may have gone to the north. He returned to the island at least once in the decade to come, and there is evidence for rebuilding and repair work at forts on the Wall under his command. He died in York in 306, and the army proclaimed his son Constantine as emperor, prompting a new civil war. It is probable that Constantine campaigned in the north early in his reign, for he took the names Britannicus Maximus, but later much of his reign was spent preparing for and fighting civil wars, as he steadily brought the entire empire under his sole control. One of his sons came to Britain in the winter of 342–3 and it is likely that there was more fighting. The historian and former army officer Ammianus Marcellinus tells us that in 360 Picts and Scots (the latter a group who appear to have come to Scotland from Ireland) broke 'the peace that had been agreed upon... laying waste the regions near the frontiers, so that fear seized the provincials'. Four units of *comitatenses* – at most a few thousand men – and an experienced commander were sent to deal with the problem. In 367–8 the same two groups, joined by the previously unknown Attacotti in a so-called 'conspiracy of barbarians', again raided the province, ranging far to the south, killing one Roman commander and capturing another. They were aided by information supplied by the army's own scouts, who were subsequently disbanded, but once again a proven officer – in this case the father of the future emperor Theodosius – was sent with four units to restore the situation. Both campaigns suggest weak frontier defences allowing a rapid increase in the scale and frequency of raiding until fairly modest reinforcement drove the attackers out of the province.[33]

In 382 Magnus Maximus, originally from Spain and now the *dux* (a late Roman military rank) commanding the troops in Britain, fought a campaign against the Picts and Scots who had attacked the province. Encouraged by this victory, in the following year he declared himself emperor in direct challenge to Gratian, the emperor in the western provinces. Maximus invaded Gaul, but it is clear that he had already secured the support of many of Gratian's senior officers. When the armies met near Lutetia (modern Paris), there were a few minor skirmishes before Gratian's army defected en masse. The defeated emperor fled, but was caught and executed, leaving Maximus in charge of all

Two legionaries from the early third century show the profound changes in military equipment and dress with a merging of styles between legionaries and auxiliaries.

provinces north of the Alps. Maximus hoped to be recognized by Theodosius, emperor in the eastern provinces, and there was a lull of several years while they negotiated. In 387 Maximus once again resorted to force and overran Italy. Theodosius responded the following year, launching a rapid offensive; Maximus was defeated, taken captive and beheaded. There was some more fighting before his supporters were suppressed and the western provinces once again secured by Theodosius and his two young co-rulers.

This episode forms the background for Kipling's story of the centurion Parnesius, who is tasked with holding the Wall even though the bulk of the army in Britain has been led away to fight in the civil war. In fact we do not know what happened in the north during Maximus's bid for power, although it is clear that he must have drawn away many soldiers from the provincial garrison. Some inevitably died in battle or from disease in the civil war, while others may never have been sent back to their bases in Britain. Any civil war weakened the defences of all the empire's frontiers, and the consequences were inevitably worse for provinces directly involved in the fighting. Britain had a strong garrison for its size, so that the men who controlled it were often confident enough to make a bid for imperial power. As an island, it also offered a fairly secure base and made it difficult for emperors based on the continent to launch a quick counterattack in the early days when a new regime was especially vulnerable. Even so, it was not always easy for an aspiring emperor to control all of the troops stationed there.

Between 406 and 407 no fewer than three usurpers to the imperial throne were proclaimed in Britain, the first two swiftly perishing at the hands of their own officers. The third, Constantius III, gathered enough soldiers to invade Gaul and for a short while held sway over a sizeable part of the western empire. Influential men left behind in Britain clearly felt neglected, for they rebelled and rejected his rule. A late, and not always very reliable, source claims that in 410 a delegation from Britain went to the Emperor Honorius in Italy. They asked for help against barbarian attacks, only to be told 'to fend for themselves', according to the Byzantine writer Zosimus. By this time it is clear that the Roman state had ceased to function in Britain, so that effectively it had ceased to be part of the empire. Several years before this, newly minted currency had stopped reaching the island in any significant quantities, which is a clear sign of the end of military and civilian administration. Whatever the precise details of the process, formal rule of Britain by the Western Roman Empire ended early in the fifth century.

Over time the Roman empire's capacity to fight fires on several frontiers simultaneously had declined, rotting away over generations of internal power struggles and civil war. Provinces were lost and not recovered, with no single event triggering the decline or marking the point of no return. The impression from the archaeological record is of units on Hadrian's Wall continuing to do their job throughout the fourth and into the early years of the fifth century. Occasionally new units arrived to reinforce the troops stationed there, but there were also periods of weakness, and these may well have been more common than in the past. Even so there was no permanent collapse, and the Wall was maintained under Roman control until the very end of the province. As the empire declined, so did its capacity to maintain the army and garrison distant provinces. Civil wars again and again took soldiers away from Britain, and disrupted the administration.

By the fourth century the culture of senior army officers and senior civil servants was one of suspicion and fear, knowing that accusations of disloyalty to the emperor would most likely be met by torture and death for themselves and their families. On more than one occasion, loyal and capable commanders felt that they had no option but to rebel because their very success had made the emperor consider them as a threat. It was not a climate encouraging talent or initiative, and the permanent insecurity and suspicion of officers and officials at all levels contributed to an inertia at the heart of government which made it hard for the empire to marshal and direct its still substantial resources to deal with problems on the frontiers. It is hard to say whether or not the threats from outside the empire had grown greater, but the ability to cope with them had certainly declined. Every successful raid encouraged more attacks, a snowball effect that rapidly magnified the problems faced by the imperial authorities. Given the chance, Roman armies were still very efficient, better equipped, disciplined and trained than their opponents and usually able to defeat them in battle. Yet the long decay of the administrative, financial and logistical structures of the army and state underpinning this effectiveness made it rarer and rarer for provincial armies to reach such high standards. It was often easier in the short term to hire allied warriors from the same sort of tribes and leaders who were attacking the empire. Controlling such forces proved hard, not least because constant power struggles within the empire meant that it was easy for such bands to find themselves on the losing side of a civil war and suddenly without a paymaster.

Saxons from northern Germany are said to have raided Britain in 367. By the beginning of the fourth century there was an army officer with the title Count of the Saxon Shore (*comes litoris Saxonici per Britannias*) commanding bases along the eastern and southern coasts. Opinion is divided as to whether he was there to defend against Saxon attacks from the sea or whether he commanded Saxon allies serving with the Roman army who garrisoned these bases. By this time the units on the Wall were part of another division of the army, led by the *dux Britanniarum*. Britain was split into four or five provinces. An impression of

overleaf: Sycamore Gap to the west of Housesteads is one of the most famous spots along the Wall. It even appears in the Kevin Costner movie *Robin Hood: Prince of Thieves.*

Two soldiers typical of the garrison of the Wall by the end of the third century and for the rest of its life.

insecurity is fed by the fact that every significant town on the island acquired defensive walls during the fourth century, if not before. As so often, the evidence is so poor that we simply cannot gauge the scale and frequency of raiding or those areas most affected. Many attacks seem to have come by sea, which was no doubt easier than attempting to cross the Wall. The sixteen-year-old St Patrick was abducted from western Britain by pirates from Ireland sometime in the fifth century, although we do not know whether this occurred before or after the end of Roman rule. As we have seen, the details of precisely when and how Britain ceased permanently to be part of the empire are now lost. One source claims that representatives from British communities appealed unsuccessfully for aid from one of the western emperors in the middle of the fifth century. There was also continued contact through the Catholic Church for some time. The impression is that the former British provinces split into a number of separate states led by kings or warlords. These may often have been hostile to their neighbours, fighting on a smaller scale the same sort of power struggles and civil wars that had ripped the Roman empire apart.

What happened on Hadrian's Wall in these last decades is even less clear. At South Shields two skeletons with traces of wounds were discovered and dated to the early fifth century. It appears that they lay exposed for some time before they were buried in a pit in the courtyard of the old *praetorium*. This violent episode, whatever its nature and scale, did not bring a final end to life at the fort and some buildings remained in use. There is also evidence for continued occupation in several forts along Hadrian's Wall for at least a few generations. Someone had enough power on a local scale to maintain these in a reasonable state of repair, and presumably kept armed followers to act as garrisons. Opinion is divided over whether these were the descendants of the old garrisons and leaders, or chieftains from the new kingdoms that began to emerge. Whatever their origins, they are more likely to have acted like the warbands of tribal noblemen than units of a formal army.

At Birdoswald, the collapsed granary building was used as foundations for a large timber building, with old flagstones and other stones used as flooring. The nearby gateway was repaired, and another big timber building was raised on the site of the old granary. Both this and its predecessor look more like a chieftain's feasting hall than a Roman military building, and generally the fifth-century occupation tends to resemble a hillfort rather than the base of professional soldiers. However, the transition may have been gradual. The Wall itself and its milecastles were occupied and in good repair for most of the fourth century, but there is no hint that this continued in an organized way afterwards. Power and society had become much more local. Perhaps some communities still liked to think of themselves as 'Roman' and civilized, and did their best to maintain old practices, so that there was no abrupt change in lifestyle.

Yet change there was over time, and as wealth and stability faded so did the technical capacity and skill they supported. The remaining towns of the old provinces shrank in size, the villas and other communities declined. No one was able to build new s or aqueducts any more, and before long they were incapable of maintaining the ones already in existence. An organized professional fighting force like the Roman army requires the support of immense political power and huge resources to function. These no longer existed in Britain and in time throughout the Western provinces, although pockets may have remained for a while. The biography of St Severinus, who was active in the Danubian provinces in the fifth century, tells of an isolated garrison still doing its best to perform its duty even though they had not received pay or orders for a considerable time. The unit sent a delegation to Italy in search of both these things, but the men encountered a band of barbarians and were massacred.[34]

Over the course of the fifth century the influence and power of groups of Angles, Saxons and other Germanic tribes increased. By this time it will come as no surprise to readers that the evidence for this is poor, often confused, and its interpretation furiously debated by scholars. What is not in dispute is that over time Roman law was replaced by Germanic law, the Latin language by Anglo-Saxon, Christianity by a Germanic form of paganism, and the kingdoms that emerged in the post-Roman period were replaced by new ones ruled by Anglo-Saxon dynasties, which centuries later would combine to form England. The Roman empire had gone, and little of its legacy was left in Britain except in the western lands like Wales and Cornwall where British kingdoms endured. It survived only in place-names like 'chester' and 'caster', both from the Latin 'castra' or camp, and more dramatically in the remains of the roads and monumental buildings left from the Roman era. Hadrian's Wall was the greatest of these, but over time it and all the others crumbled. Once Catholic missionaries converted the Anglo-Saxons to Christianity, the drive of kings and aristocrats to raise up ever more grand churches and monasteries encouraged the population to see the Wall and other old Roman buildings as little more than ready sources of building stone. Much of Hadrian's Wall was deliberately taken apart and its stone put to new uses as life went on in the lands and people farmed, tended their herds and flocks, worshipped in new ways, and fought new wars and squabbles.

Lying close to – and in part on – what would become the border between England and Scotland, the lands around Hadrian's Wall have seen a good deal of warfare and violence since the end of the Roman era. In the sixteenth century in particular these were the haunts of the Border Reivers, who raided and feuded for generations, exploiting the weakness of central authority. In

1745, Bonnie Prince Charlie came south with his Jacobite army of Highlanders and Lowlanders, Irish and Scottish regular troops supplied by the French, and soon some English volunteers. Their route was down the west coast, and General Wade, commanding the government forces at Newcastle, was unable to march fast enough to Carlisle to block their path because there was not a road good enough for his artillery and transport. This failure prompted the construction of a new road in 1752 so that the same thing could not happen again. Unsurprisingly the best route lay for many miles along the line of Hadrian's Wall, the remnants of which were demolished in the process, down to the foundations that were used by the road. Today, as you drive along the B6318, you are driving along Wade's road on the line of the Wall, often with the ditch on one side and the Vallum on the other.

History never stands still, and priorities change as well as memories. It was not that long after the end of the Roman era that idea of what the Wall had been became confused – that is, when people bothered to think about it at all. Writing near the middle of the sixth century, the British monk Gildas gave a muddled version of its history, claiming that it was raised after the end of the Roman province. In this version the Britons first built a turf wall to repel the Picts and Scots, but when this proved ineffective they sought aid from the Roman empire. This led to an expedition and the construction of a more effective stone wall, which gave brief respite until its British garrison proved too weak to hold it. In the eighth century Bede gave a marginally more accurate account, at least associating the first construction of a wall with Septimius Severus, but he was influenced by Gildas or a common source and has the fifth-century Britons building first the Antonine Wall of turf and then a stone wall with aid and encouragement from the Romans.[35]

During the Middle Ages there was confusion, but over time a gradual acceptance that there had been a great wall built by

Severus, even if this was often associated with the threat posed by Picts and Scots. During the Renaissance scholars began to piece the story together from the meagre mentions in the literary sources and the knowledge that a great feature was still visible on the ground. In 1584 the German traveller Lupold von Wedel saw 'a ditch, which the Emperor Severus had ordered to be made to separate Scotland from England, and the foundation of a wall, which the Emperor Hadrianus erected to hinder the Scotch from invading England, as they used to do before'. Curiously this reversed the belief of contemporary scholars that the turf wall – in fact the Vallum – was Hadrian's work, and that Severus built the Wall in stone. This probably reflects the confused opinions of his guides. It was only in later centuries that antiquarians began to unravel the story of Hadrian's Wall – a task that is still not complete.[36]

Visiting
Hadrian's Wall

The central section of Hadrian's Wall is the most visited for a very good reason. The forts at Housesteads, Chesters and Birdoswald give a good impression of such bases and each has its own museum, as does the civilian town at Corbridge. Vindolanda (Chesterholm) deserves at least half a day, for its site and ongoing excavations during the summer months, and also for the wonderful museum. Priorities for excavation change year by year, but the excellent website run by the Vindolanda Trust will provide details of recent and current activity: http://www. vindolanda.com/. Its sister site, the Roman Army Museum at Carvoran, is also worth a visit if you have the time.

There is good walking with spectacular views of the countryside throughout this area. The walk for all or part of the way between Steel Rigg (where there is a car park) and Housesteads is a particular favourite of mine. Not only is the landscape spectacular, but it also gives a very good introduction to the Wall, with the excavated milecastles 39 and 37 and the unexcavated 38, as well as the additional turret at Peel Gap. If you begin the walk at Steel Rigg, the hardest part comes a few minutes later when scrambling up the steps and rocks at Peel Gap, which can be slippery in wet weather. If you are capable of this, then the rest of the walk should present no difficulties if you go at your own pace. It's also worth stopping frequently to admire the views and to turn and look behind you and see the Wall running across the rolling land to the west. Walltown Crags are another favourite stopping place for those wanting a quick look at the Wall, and these are also well signposted and provided with a car park. Walkers eager not to retrace their steps may want to take advantage of the bus service connected to many of the main sites: http://hadrianswallcountry.co.uk/travel/bus.

If time permits, milecastle 48 at Poltross Burn is rewarding, as is the mithraeum at Carrawburgh: the narrow temple to the eastern god has casts of the wattle-and-daub inner walls and copies of the three altars found there (the originals are now in the Great North Museum in Newcastle). The fort of Carrawburgh shows visitors what an unexcavated fort looks like, providing a good contrast with sites that have seen more work. There is a car park at both sites, although watch carefully for the sign to Poltross Burn as it is a sharp turn to the left, just before the railway bridge, when approaching from the east. Carrawburgh is on the military way built by General Wade (the B6318), as is Limestone Corner. A drive along the road will give good views of the Vallum and ditch and take you past many of the key sites, so is a good option for those without the time or inclination to do a lot of walking. Even so, sturdy footwear is a good idea for stops at the various sites. The path down to the mithraeum at Carrawburgh is usually muddy throughout the year.

In the east, a visitor relying on public transport could easily fill a day in and around Newcastle, visiting Wallsend and South Shields, each of which has reconstructed buildings and a museum, and the Great North Museum in the city centre, which houses a major gallery of material from Hadrian's Wall. In the west, the Tullie House Museum in Carlisle is good, and on the Cumbrian coast the Senhouse Museum at Maryport is also rewarding.

For walkers with more time and energy, there is the Hadrian's Wall Path running from coast to coast for 84 miles (135 km). The beauty of much of the countryside make this a great pleasure even for those with little interest in the archaeology and history of the region. Several good guidebooks are available and there are also plenty of details online, for instance at http://hadrianswallcountry.co.uk/walking/hadrians-wall-path-national-trail. Be prepared for all weathers, even in the summer.

overleaf: The bath-house at Chesters was situated outside the fort next to the North Tyne, close to where it was crossed by a substantial arched Roman bridge.

Suggestions for
Further Reading

The best single-volume survey of Hadrian's Wall remains D. J. Breeze and B. Dobson, *Hadrian's Wall* (fourth edition, 2000). There are plenty of decent guides to the Hadrian's Wall Path, but any serious visitor should also take D. J. Breeze, *J. Collingwood Bruce's Handbook to the Roman Wall* (fourteenth edition, 2006).

For those wishing to study the evidence and approaches to its interpretation in more detail, then M. F. A. Symonds and D. J. P. Mason (eds), *Frontiers of Knowledge. A Research Framework for Hadrian's Wall, Part of the Frontiers of the Roman Empire World Heritage Site. Vol. I. Resource Assessment* (2009) provides an excellent starting place. There are very good collections of papers in P. T. Bidwell (ed.), *Understanding Hadrian's Wall* (2008), P. T. Bidwell and N. Hodgson (eds), *The Roman Army in Northern England* (2009), and R. Collins and M. Symonds (eds), *Breaking Down Boundaries. Hadrian's Wall in the 21st Century. Journal of Roman Archaeology Supplementary Series* 93 (2013). Another good and insightful survey of the evidence comes in N. Hodgson, *Hadrian's Wall 1999–2009. A Summary of Excavation and Research Prepared for the Thirteenth Pilgrimage of Hadrian's Wall, 8–14 August 2009* (2009). Those wishing to place the Wall in the context of Rome's other frontiers would do well to look at D. J. Breeze, *The Frontiers of Imperial Rome* (2011).

On more specific topics, P. Hill, *The Construction of Hadrian's Wall* (2006) is the most accessible version of the analysis of an author who has revolutionized understanding of the practical aspects of building and maintaining Hadrian's Wall. J. Poulter, *The Planning of Roman Roads and Walls in Northern Britain* (2010), similarly presents for the general reader his ground-breaking approach to understanding the process of laying out Hadrian's Wall. R. Collins, *Hadrian's Wall and the End of Empire: The Roman Frontier in the 4th and 5th Centuries* (2012) is the most detailed examination of the later years of the Wall. G. B. D. Jones and D. J. Woolliscroft, *Hadrian's Wall from the Air* (2001) offers a fresh and well-illustrated perspective on the Wall and its sites. For the history of study of Hadrian's Wall, see D. J. Breeze, *Hadrian's Wall: A History of Archaeological Thought* (2014), and W. D. Shannon, *Ille Murus Famosus (That Famous Wall). Depictions and Descriptions of Hadrian's Wall before Camden* (2007) covers the medieval and Renaissance periods in detail. On the Roman army in general, my own *The Complete Roman Army* (2003) and D. J. Breeze, *The Roman Army* (2016) offer introductions.

A good deal of research on the Wall is published in *Archaeologia Aeliana*, the journal of the Society of Antiquaries in Newcastle-upon-Tyne. Notable recent articles include:

D. J. BREEZE, 'Did Hadrian design Hadrian's Wall?', *AA 5th Series* 38 (2009), pp. 87–103
——— 'The Vallum of Hadrian's Wall', *AA 5th Series* 44 (2015), pp. 1–29

D. J. BREEZE AND P. HILL, 'The foundations of Hadrian's stone wall', *AA 5th Series* 42 (2013), pp. 101–14

M. CORBY, 'Hadrian's Wall and the defence of north Britain', *AA 5th Series* 39 (2010), pp. 9–13

B. DOBSON, 'The function of Hadrian's Wall', *AA 5th Series* 14 (1986), pp. 1–30

J. GILLAM, 'The frontier after Hadrian – a history of the problem', *AA 5th Series* 2 (1974), pp. 1–16

E. GRAAFSTAL, 'Hadrian's haste: a priority programme for the Wall', *AA 5th Series* 41 (2012), pp. 123–84

M. SYMONDS, 'The construction order of the milecastles on Hadrian's Wall,' *AA 5th Series* 34 (2005), pp. 67–81

H. WELFARE, 'Causeways, at milecastles, across the ditch of Hadrian's Wall,' *AA 5th Series* 28 (2000), pp. 13–25
——— 'Variation in the form of the ditch, and of its equivalents, on Hadrian's Wall,' *AA 5th Series* 33 (2004), pp. 9–23

This is a very short and incomplete list of the copious scholarship on Hadrian's Wall, but these works in turn provide many references and should allow those who wish to delve more deeply into the subject to do so.

The University of Newcastle runs a free online course about Hadrian's Wall, and details may be found at https://www. futurelearn.com/courses/hadrians-wall. Also of great interest is the Hadrianic Society: http://www.hadrianicsociety.com/.

overleaf: Reconstruction of the fort gateway at South Shields which gives an idea of the imposing entrances to Roman army bases.

Chronology

55 BC
Julius Caesar raids south-eastern Britain.

54 BC
Julius Caesar launches a larger expedition to south-eastern Britain, but leaves before the end of the year.

27 BC–AD 14
Augustus becomes Rome's first emperor. Although the poets write excitedly about the conquest of Britain, he does not attempt this.

41–54
Reign of Emperor Claudius.

43
Emperor Claudius sends a large army to invade Britain. Over the next few years the southe ast is overrun and occupied by Rome. Many communities and leaders welcome the Romans and ally with them, while others fight, but are overcome.

54–68
Reign of Emperor Nero.

60–1
Rebellion led by Boudica causes widespread destruction in the south. She is defeated and the revolt crushed with considerable savagery; there is never again a rebellion against Roman rule in southern Britain.

c.72–3
The Romans build a fort at Carlisle. This is part of wider occupation of what will become northern England.

78–84

Governorship of Julius Agricola and a period of aggressive campaigning in what will become Scotland. This culminates in a victory at the battle of Mons Graupius (location unknown). Bases are built in the coastal plain of south-eastern Scotland north of the River Forth, including the legionary fortress at Inchtuthil.

c.86–7

Bases north of the Forth are abandoned by the Roman army as the garrison of Britain is reduced from four to three legions.

98–117

Reign of Emperor Trajan. The major military operations of this period are on the Danube and later in the east. Little is known about Britain in these years, and the garrison was probably reduced to two legions. There are hints of some outbreaks of warfare in northern Britain.

c.106

The Roman army abandons most of its remaining bases in southern Scotland. A line of forts is occupied along the line of the Stanegate Road, just south of where Hadrian's Wall will be built. It is not clear when the road itself was built.

117–38

Reign of Emperor Hadrian. He abandons Trajan's conquests in the east and oversees a period of stability and consolidation on the frontiers. Much of his reign is spent touring the provinces. Trouble in northern Britain is attested at the start of his reign and at least one other conflict probably occurred there during his reign.

122

Hadrian visits Britain. Legio VI Victrix is added to the provincial garrison. At some point before or during his stay Hadrian orders the construction of Hadrian's Wall.

138–61

Reign of Antoninus Pius. Unlike Hadrian, Antoninus Pius spends his entire reign in Italy. Early on in his reign, there may well have been a major war in northern Britain. The decision is made to decommission Hadrian's Wall and the army constructs the Antonine Wall on the Forth–Clyde line.

158

Building work attested on Hadrian's Wall. Around this time the Antonine Wall is abandoned – either late in the reign of Antoninus Pius or early in the reign of his successor, Marcus Aurelius. Hadrian's Wall once again becomes the main component of the frontier.

161–80

Reign of Marcus Aurelius. During his reign the empire is subject to successive outbreaks of plague which results in a heavy death toll. There is also a spate of serious warfare on the Danubian frontier. Trouble in northern Britain is likely early in his reign and perhaps later on.

180–92

Reign of Commodus. Trouble in northern Britain, resulting in at least one serious defeat and the death of a legate before the situation is restored.

184

Coins issued commemorating a victory in Britain.

197–211

Reign of Septimius Severus, who is the victor in a prolonged civil war. Severus spends much of his reign consolidating his hold on power. There was a major attack on the province from tribes to the north at some point early in his reign.

208–11

Septimius Severus leads a major expedition to Britain and campaigns against the Caledonians. He dies at York.

THIRD CENTURY

Almost nothing is known about events in northern Britain for the remainder of the century.

293–305

Constantius, the Caesar (or junior emperor in the West) campaigns in Britain on more than one occasion, dying at York.

306–37

Reign of Emperor Constantine, who in a succession of civil wars gains control of the entire empire. He converts to Christianity, ending centuries of sporadic persecution of the religion.

314

Constantine takes the title Britannicus Maximus, which may hint at a successful war in Britain.

360

Picts and Scots raid northern Britain.

367

Picts, Scots and a group called the Attacotti, about whom little is known, launch major raids on the province of Britain. A significant proportion of Rome's scouts and spies collaborate with them. One Roman commander is killed in a heavy defeat, but eventually the situation is restored.

382

Magnus Maximus campaigns against Picts and Scots after a renewed burst of raiding. His victory encourages him to declare himself emperor and he is defeated and killed in Italy six years later.

410

Traditional date for the end of Roman rule in Britain. The reality is less neat, but from around 407 no new coinage arrives in Britain, suggesting an end to the formal administration and payment of officials and soldiers. Without this infrastructure Britain effectively ceases to be a province.

overleaf: A reconstruction of a stretch of Hadrian's Wall was built next to the foundations of the Wall near the site at Wallsend and showing the position of obstacles on the berm.

Appendix

The known and probable garrisons of the forts on Hadrian's Wall (after Breeze and Dobson (2000)

FORT	SECOND CENTURY	THIRD CENTURY	C.400
Wallsend	CE? Cohors II Nerviorum CR	Cohors IV Lingonum eq.	Cohors IV Lingonum
Newcastle	?	Cohors I Ulpia Traiana Cugernorum CR	Cohors Prima Cornoviorum
Benwell	Ala? Cohors I Vangionum mil. eq.	Ala I Asturum	Ala I Asturum
Rudchester	CE?	?	Cohors Prima Frixagorum (or Frisiavorum)
Halton Chesters	CE?	Ala Sabiniana	
Chesters	Ala Augusta ob virtutem appellata	Ala II Asturum	Ala II Asturum
Carrawburgh	CE?	Cohors I Batavorum eq.	Cohors I Batavorum eq.
Housesteads	CM?	Cohors I Tungrorum mil Numerus Hnaudifridi Cuneus Frisiorum	Cohors I Tungrorum
Vindolanda	Cohors II Nerviorum CR?	Cohors IV Gallorum eq.	Cohors IV Gallorum

Great Chesters	Cohors VI Nerviorum	Cohors II Asturum	Cohors II Asturum
	Cohors ? Raetorum	Raeti Gaesati (or Raetian spearman)	
Carvoran	Cohors I Hamiorum sag.	Cohors II Delmatarum eq.	Cohors II Asturum Delmatarum
Birdoswald	Cohors I Tungrorum mil.?	Cohors I Aelia Dacorum mil. Venatores Bannienses	Cohors I Aelia Dacorum
Castlesteads	Cohors IV Gallorum eq.?	Cohors II Tungrorum eq. CL	?
Stanwix	Ala Petriana?	Ala Augusta Petriana bis torquata CR	Ala Augusta
Burgh-by-Sands	CE or CM?	Cohors I Nervana Germanorum mil. eq. Numerus Maurorum Aurelianorum Cuneus Frisionum Aballavensium	Numerus Maurorum Aurelianorum
Drumburgh	?	?	?
Bowness-on-Solway		CM eq?	CM?

OUTPOST AND SUPPORTING FORTS

South Shields	C?	Cohors V Gallorum	Numerus barcariorum Tigrisiensium (or bargemen from the Tigris?)
Birrens	Cohors II Tungrorum mil. eq.	Abandoned	Abandoned

Netherby	?	Cohors I Aelia Hispanorum eq.	Abandoned
Bewcastle	Cohors I Dacorum mil. eq.	CM?	Abandoned
High Rochester	Cohors I Lingounum eq.	Cohors I fida Vardullorum CR mil.	Abandoned
	Cohors I Dac ... ?	Exploratores (or scouts) Bremenienses	
Risingham	Cohors IV Gallorum eq.	Cohors I Vangionum mil. eq.	Abandoned
		Vexillatio Raetorum gaesatorum	
		Exploratores Habitancenses	

KEY:

C = cohort

CE = cohors equitata

CL = civium Latinorum (of Latin citizens)

CM = cohors milliaria

CR = civium romanorum (of Roman citizens)

eq. = equitata (mixed cohort)

mil. = Milliaria (double strength)

Acknowledgements

A s usual, I must thank the family and friends, and especially Kevin Powell, who read drafts of this book and did a great deal to improve its clarity. This book draws on the work of many dedicated scholars of Hadrian's Wall and the Roman army, including all those listed under further reading, and my understanding of the subject has been shaped by reading and talking to many of them. I am not an archaeologist but a historian, and most of my work has been concerned with the Roman army more generally rather than Hadrian's Wall. Such is the enthusiasm of Wall scholars that they are always eager to discuss the subject and share their insights. I must particularly thank David Breeze and Ian Haynes, who took the time to read and comment in detail on this manuscript. Their contributions have made this a much better book, although any faults that remain are my own. Throughout my work on this book I kept in mind a comment of the late Brian Dobson, who wrote that 'again and again as we strive to express some truth about the Wall we find that it has already been said, better and clearer... If we ever imagine we glimpse some new truth about Hadrian's Wall, it is simply because we stand on the shoulders of giants'.

Notes

1 R. Kipling, *Puck of Pook's Hill* (1906, quoted from Penguin Popular Classics, 1994), p. 124.

2 Scriptores Historia Augusta, *Hadrian* 11.2; for *Vallum Aelium* see R. Tomlin, *Britannia* 35 (2004), pp. 344–5 (Loeb translation).

3 Cicero, *Letters to Atticus* 4.17 (Loeb translation).

4 Tacitus, *Annals* 1.11.

5 Horace, *Odes* 3.5.2–4 (Loeb translation, slightly modified); Strabo, *Geography* 2.5.8.

6 A. Bowman and J. Thomas, *The Vindolanda Writing-Tablets. Vol. II* (1994), 154, line 23, and 164 for the *Brittunculi*; A. Birley, 'A new tombstone from Vindolanda', *Britannia* 29 (1998), pp. 299–306.

7 For a good survey of the evidence for the peoples of the north, see I. Armit, *Celtic Scotland* (3rd edition, 2016).

8 Historia Augusta, *Hadrian* 10.2–11.1 (Loeb translation).

9 R. Collingwood, R. Wright and R. Tomlin (eds), *Roman Inscriptions in Britain* (1995), 1471 and 1475. This work is now available online at https://romaninscriptionsofbritain.org/.

10 Pausanias, *Description of Greece* 8.43.4.

11 Marcus Aurelius, *Meditations* 7.36, 8.5 (Wordsworth Classics of World Literature Series, trans. R. Hard, 1997).

12 Dio 73.1.1, 8.2, 6 (Loeb translation).

13 Dio 73.9.1–4, Historia Augusta, *Pertinax* 3.5–10 (Loeb translation).

14 Dio 76.9.4 (Loeb translation). On coin hoards, see F. Hunter, '*Denarius* hoards beyond the frontier. A Scottish case study', in A. Morillo, N. Hanl and E. Martín (eds), *Limes XX. Estudios Sobre La Frontera Romana Roman Frontier Studies. Vol. 1* (2009), pp. 1619–30.

15 Bede, *Ecclesiastical History of the English People* 1.12.

16 Some archaeologists now question whether we have exaggerated the extent to which the *vicus* outside an army camp was truly granted formal status as an independent community. Instead they use the phrase 'extra mural settlement' for the area beyond the ramparts of a fort. In a general overview like this it is impossible to cover this debate, and I have preferred to use *vicus* instead of the longer phrase.

17 On the Antonine Wall and in some other cases, such as Newstead, bath-houses were constructed inside forts, or at least inside an annexe to the main fort, which was also protected by rampart and ditch. Sadly in a book of this length, there is not space for a detailed comparison between Hadrian's Wall and the Antonine Wall.

18 Ammianus Marcellinus 27.2.11.

19 A. Bowman and J. Thomas, *The Vindolanda Writing-Tablets. Vol. III* (2003), 574.

20 R. Fink, *Roman Military Records on Papyrus* (1971), 87, 99, *P. Oxy.* 39; R. Tomlin, 'Making the machine work', in A. Goldsworthy and I. Haynes (eds), *The Roman Army as a Community. Journal of Roman Archaeology Supplementary Series* 34 (1999), pp. 127–38, with M. Speidel, 'The missing weapons at Carlisle', *Britannia* 38 (2007), pp. 237–9, esp. 238–9 on the *subarmales*.

21 A. Bowman and J. Thomas, *The Vindolanda Writing-Tablets. Vol. II* (1994) 154, 225, 25.

22 M. P. Speidel, *Emperor Hadrian's speeches to the African army – a new text* (2006), pp. 12–15.

23 Josephus, *The Jewish War* 3. 73–6 (Loeb translation).

24 A. Bowman and J. Thomas, *The Vindolanda Writing-Tablets.Vol. III* (2003), 628.

25 A. Bowman and J. Thomas, *The Vindolanda Writing-Tablets. Vol. II* (1994), 301.

26 The skeletons at Housesteads were found at an early excavation and are no longer available for analysis, which means that we must register a degree of caution about the estimates of their age and gender, but the presence beneath the floor still make murder the most likely explanation.

27 *Roman Inscriptions in Britain* 1065.

28 *Roman Inscriptions in Britain* 1062, 1064, 1180, 1181, 1182.

29 *Roman Inscriptions in Britain* 829 from Maryport.

30 *Roman Inscriptions in Britain* 1544.

31 *Roman Inscriptions in Britain* 1041 for Silvanus, for Cocidius see 985–9, 993.

32 *Roman Inscriptions in Britain* 1142.

33 Ammianus Marcellinus 20.1.1, 27.8.1–9.

34 Eugippius, *The Life of St. Severinus* 20.1–2.

35 Gildas, *The Ruin of Britain* 1.15–19, Bede, *Ecclesiastical History* 1.12.

36 G. von Bülow, 'Journey through England and Scotland made by Lupold von Wedel in the years 1584 and 1585', *Transactions of the Royal Historical Society* 9 (1894), p. 239. I am very grateful to Christopher Sparey-Green for bringing this reference to my attention.

Index